Introduction to the Series

...e seminar method of teaching is being used increasingly. It is a v...
...learning in smaller groups through discussion, designed both to...
...ay from and to supplement the basic lecture techniques. To...
...cessful, the members of a seminar must be informed — or else, in...
...kind phrase of a cynic — it can be a 'pooling of ignorance'. ...
...pter in the textbook of English or European history by its nat...
...not provide material in this depth, but at the same time the...
...demic work may be too long and perhaps too advanced.

...For this reason we have invited practising teachers to contrib...
...t studies on specialised aspects of British and European hist...
...these special needs in mind. For this series the authors have b...
...d to provide, in addition to their basic analysis, a full selection...
...mentary material of all kinds and an up-to-date and comprehens...
...ography. Both these sections are referred to in the text, but i...
...d that they will prove to be valuable teaching and learning aid...
...selves.

...on the System of References:
...d number in round brackets (**5**) in the text refers the reader to...
...ponding entry in the Bibliography section at the end of the bo...

...d number in square brackets, preceded by 'doc' [**docs 6,8**] re...
...ader to the corresponding items in the section of Documer...
...follows the main text.

PATRICK RICHARDS...
General Edi...

1776
The American
Challenge
R. C. Birch

LONGMAN GROUP LIMITED
London

Associated companies, branches and
representatives throughout the world

First published 1976

ISBN 0 582 35217 7

Printed in Great Britain by
Whitstable Litho Ltd., Whitstable, Kent.

Set in IBM Press Roman by
Type Practitioners Ltd, Sevenoaks, Kent

Contents

Acknowledgements

We are grateful to the following for permission to reproduce copyright material:

A. & C. Black Ltd for extracts from *Debate on the American Revolution* edited by Max Beloff in The British Political Tradition Series; Macmillan Publishers Ltd for an extract from *The Revolution in America* edited by J.R. Pole; Oxford University Press for extracts from *Sources and Documents illustrating the American Revolution, 1764-1788* edited by Samuel Eliot Morison 2nd edition 1929; and University of North Carolina Press for extracts from *Prologue to Revolution* by Morgan.

The cover illustration is reproduced by permission of the Radio Times Hulton Picture Library.

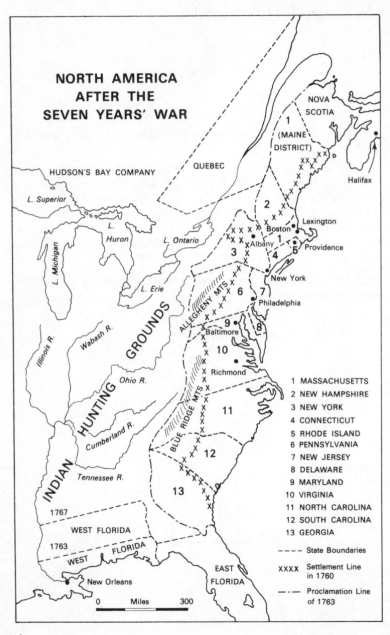

NORTH AMERICA
AFTER THE
SEVEN YEARS' WAR

HUDSON'S BAY COMPANY

QUEBEC

NOVA SCOTIA

1
(MAINE DISTRICT)

Halifax

L. Superior

L. Huron

L. Michigan

L. Ontario

L. Erie

Illinois R.

Wabash R.

Ohio R.

Cumberland R.

Tennessee R.

INDIAN HUNTING GROUNDS

ALLEGHENY MTS

BLUE RIDGE MTS

2

1
Boston

Lexington

Albany

Providence

4

5

New York

6

7

Philadelphia

9
Baltimore

8

10

Richmond

11

12

13

1767

WEST FLORIDA

1763

WEST FLORIDA

New Orleans

EAST FLORIDA

0   Miles   300

1 MASSACHUSETTS
2 NEW HAMPSHIRE
3 NEW YORK
4 CONNECTICUT
5 RHODE ISLAND
6 PENNSYLVANIA
7 NEW JERSEY
8 DELAWARE
9 MARYLAND
10 VIRGINIA
11 NORTH CAROLINA
12 SOUTH CAROLINA
13 GEORGIA

- - - - State Boundaries

XXXX Settlement Line
in 1760

—·—·— Proclamation Line
of 1763

PART ONE

The Background

1 Introduction

Few events bear such testimony to the infinite variety of historical interpretation as the American Revolution; the reasons are not difficult to find. As a domestic event, and to American writers, it is the period of the first growth of American society, and their reading of it has invariably been affected by their view of that society as it has matured; in few other cases has Croce's dictum that every true history is contemporary history been so relevant. Other historians have looked outwards, finding their main theme not so much in the making of a nation as in the decay of the old colonial system within which it grew. Yet more have applied themselves to the sequels; to the growth of worldwide free trade; to the beginning of the new imperial order which grew into Commonwealth – to some a system feverishly put together from the ruins of the old to meet the challenge of the new situation in North America after 1783, to others a halting yet continuous development from the wars with the Bourbons which had ended twenty years earlier; or to the separate evolution of democratic federal republicanism in the United States and unitary constitutional monarchy in Britain, which, although rooted in the same soil, produced absorbing variants of popular government in the western world. In the widest possible terms, the rebellion of the Thirteen Colonies has been seen as the first upthrust of the revolutionary force which, through France, was to shake the political and social foundations of Europe in the nineteenth century and give violent birth to new nations and new governments in the years that were to follow (**42,43**). The principles of the American Revolution are truly, as John Adams wrote in 1807, 'as various as the thirteen states which went through it, and in some sense as diversified as the individuals who acted in it', and it is small wonder that the search for meaning has been so assiduously followed or that so many different threads have led away from this one series of events.

Excellent surveys of the development of historical attitudes to the Revolution abound, and while no really detailed examination can be attempted in the space of one short volume, its broad outlines may be simply stated (**55,56,57**). American patriot historians of the first half of the nineteenth century, like Bancroft, found that the spirit of the Revo-

3

lution had been planted with the colonies themselves, to simmer through the years of mercantilist oppression towards a glorious explosion of liberty after 1763, and saw its purpose as the transmission of a precious inheritance of freedom. English Whig historians like George Otto Trevelyan set the victory of the Americans over a king and his ministers who were trying to subvert the glorious English Constitution, firmly in the pathway to nineteenth-century liberal reform. The growing influence of the continental school of scientific and impartial history at the end of the nineteenth century was to qualify the simple idealism of both. American 'Imperial' historians, chiefly Osgood, Beer and Andrews, produced detailed studies to suggest that the old colonial system was well-organised and even beneficially directed, and weighed upon the colonists but little (31). Namierite historians in Britain, writing later, found little evidence of deliberate tyranny in the policies of British ministers, who, absorbed in the vendettas of faction and ruled by predominantly local interests, could rarely apply any consistent national policy at all (15,16). The 'Progressive' school of roughly the same period, influenced by the new disciplines of political science and economics, and eager to see the foundation of their nation as part of the European revolutionary tradition, saw idealism as no more than the superficial expression of deeper social forces, and the Revolution in terms of the class antagonisms of the age in which they wrote; its essential origins were in the competing capitalisms of Britain and America, and its course significantly affected by a quite separate internal struggle between a conservative merchant and planting group, and the radicals and democrats who represented a different and largely unprivileged class (44,46). Thus were the heroism of Americans and the sinister intentions of Englishmen brought into perspective; the motives of men, it seemed, mattered less than the involuntary forces which inevitably tore the old colonial order apart. Separated by three thousand miles of ocean, the social and economic development of the colonies diverged radically from that of Britain, producing in them the unavoidable desire to control their own destinies; while in Britain the complexities of a developing empire would lead to a barely formulated but inescapable demand for a more centralised colonial system that would be able to deal effectively with issues much wider than those concerned with America alone. The colonists, finding themselves unable to adapt to the changing conditions within the British world, to conform to the demands of the new imperial organisation that was coming so painfully into existence, were led inevitably into an attitude of revolution.

In recent times these progressive and scientific views have lost some of their popularity. It has been suggested that in a period in which affluence gave rest to social conflict, and in which the United States took up the leadership of the free and stable world against an order which had its roots in revolutionary violence, its leaders wished to affirm, perhaps unconsciously, the idealism which gave the nation its life. Whatever the reasons, historians of the last thirty years have seen the Revolution as a successful attempt to re-establish legal and constitutional rights long cherished under the British flag, and which were not threatened until the French wars brought Englishmen to the edge of imperial reorganisation; and they have further suggested that these rights were so effectively reaffirmed precisely because a social revolution, in the absence of a landed order or an established Church, was not necessary. The Progressive school stressed the extent of the social and economic change the Revolution brought about; those who disagree, while conceding that in the vital period between 1774 and 1776 extreme radicals made all the running, have pointed to their relative absence at the end of the struggle when, in the Constitution of 1787, a markedly conservative leadership was able to give moderate foundations to the new society. A comparison with the French revolutionary tradition, in which social conflict seriously inhibited the growth of liberty, was therefore pointless (**49,50,51**).

In this revision, the older work of the Imperial school has stood up well. The most recent investigations of the colonial period reveal little evidence of a serious conflict between competing economic systems, and underlines the view that the Americans were not markedly at odds with a leniently administered mercantile organisation from which they gained considerable benefit (**28**). They produce little evidence of criticism of it in popular literature before 1763, and even carry the suggestion that the Americans were being parochial in hesitating to accept the new responsibilities of their membership of a rapidly expanding empire. Their failure in this respect, both in and after the Seven Years War, left British administrations with little alternative but to create a new imperial organisation without colonial approval. It was only at this point, when they attempted to raise a revenue to sustain it, that the constitutional quarrel began.

At the same time, different areas of recent study throw into relief the scant evidence of economic incompatibility by finding considerable traces of a lively and significant political life in the colonies before 1763, in which the English tradition of legal and constitutional freedom found pride of place. Their constitutional claims after this date were thus far from being the masks for a growing economic self-sufficiency, but were concerned overwhelmingly and sincerely with the defence of rights they already believed to be in existence; and one of the most recent works on the origins of the Revolution appeals persuasively for these ideological factors to be seen as determining essentially the course of the revolutionary struggle. The wish to preserve property from illegal taxation, to defend personal liberty against arbitrary power by the establishment of an independent judiciary and trial by jury, to gain full legislative competence for the local assemblies, and to limit the threat implied in the existence of a standing army – these were the real currency of the Revolution (**45**).

The two main issues of the revolutionary period which thus emerge – the British need for a new imperial and world position, the American determination to retain what they believed to be their constitutional rights, within it or outside it – must be placed together in any search for a satisfactory explanation. To place too great an emphasis on the political and constitutional demands of the colonists is to give less than due sympathy to the British predicament, making its administrations into caricatures of degeneracy and corruption and neglecting the depth and complexity of the factors which went to make up their policies as they groped towards a new basis for world power in which the American possessions were but one element. An assessment of the quest for a more comprehensive policy with authority enough to overcome colonial limitations is a necessary prelude to an account of the struggle for colonial rights. For it was a vital Anglo-American community that had broken down in 1763, and its informal links had failed; the mercantile system had faltered in the war conditions it was supposed to sustain, and there was growing impatience in Whitehall with the apparent unwillingness of the colonists to play a part commensurate with their growing economic importance in shouldering new responsibilities and in reaching, with Britain, towards the prizes to be won (**54**).

A dispute within the family, for this is what the American Revolution was, especially over the issue of neglected responsibilities, can be a bitter one. Both sides shared a common constitutional heritage, and against this background the attempt to reorganise the empire could be seen as little more than a species of tyranny. For the regeneration of the empire turned on the question of taxation, and the Americans refused to suffer this at the hands of any body in which they were not represented. The roots of their opposition were in England, and in the seventeenth-century, but they were opposing, after 1763, no longer the pretensions of arbitrary kingship, but the full power of a parliament which, after the victory of 1688 and its subsequent consolidation, would admit of no limits to its sovereignty. The eighteenth-century mind found it impossible to accept that sovereignty could be divided, located in not one assembly but shared between several. And while there were attempts on both sides to build bridges between these opposing points of view, to reconcile contending claims and even to look forward to a more informal imperial organisation, the prevailing eighteenth-century view of unitary government was far too strong to permit them to succeed.

It is of course a truism to suggest that the nineteenth-century conception of dominion status would have provided the solution to the American problem – although it is often forgotten that the white dominions which grew towards it had never lived within an older mercantilism. What is of more interest in respect of the need for a new imperial pattern is that when ideology had made its case, and freedom had been proclaimed, the leaders of the new American federation had themselves to meet the demands of the continental organisation they had resisted at the hands of the British. A recent study of *The Federalist,* the organ of those Americans who worked for closer unity after 1783, has shown convincingly that the demands and attitudes of the British statesmen of the 1760s are reflected all too clearly in the statements of policy made by American leaders who, over twenty years later, were faced with the great responsibility of finding a way to govern a new continent (**57**). Taxation, the defence of a frontier, economic organisation, and a programme for the interior; these were the problems of both, and, from Albany in 1754, they struggled towards a common solution. The assumptions of empire which prevailed at the end of the eighteenth century could not allow them to find it together. They were thus forced apart along a common seam, and British Commonwealth and American Federation developed separately in the years ahead. Yet they were still looking for their own solutions to the problem which had divided them before 1776, and which remains a vital issue in the modern world – that of how best to achieve an association of free peoples.

2 The Prelude

THE OLD COLONIAL PATTERN

On the eve of the Seven Years War the British occupied three distinct areas of North America. In the north Newfoundland and Nova Scotia, neither with more than a few thousand inhabitants, were little more than trading or military outposts. In the south the eight island colonies of Jamaica, Antigua, Nevis, St Kitts, Montserrat, Barbados, Bermuda and the Bahamas provided the key to British naval and economic power in the West Indies. Between them, along the American eastern seaboard, lay the thirteen separate colonies that were the heart of the transatlantic empire: Massachusetts, New Hampshire, Rhode Island, Connecticut, New York, New Jersey, Pennsylvania, Delaware, Maryland, Virginia, North and South Carolina and Georgia. Their combined population has been estimated at some one-and-a-half million, a figure which includes roughly 200,000 slaves. The first four, which together made up the provinces of New England, were still as English as the name suggests; further south the Dutch remained a strong element in New York; New Jersey and Pennsylvania had both experienced a considerable immigration by Ulster Scots in the early eighteenth century; and the latter, along with Massachusetts and the Carolinas, had seen a marked immigration from the German states. While it is too early to talk of a racial mixture, by the middle of the eighteenth century one-third of the people of the Thirteen Colonies were not of English descent, and shared few of the associations that were common to the rest.

It was also a population that had begun to move. While the colonists occupied principally a belt of land varying in width between 150 and 200 miles from the coast, in the west they were pushing into the foothills of the Appalachians, and in some parts, notably in Virginia, spilling over their watershed. They were in many places in significant contact with the Indians and had established with them a considerable trade in fur, in exchange for which they supplied guns, liquor and assorted hardware; they were also, just as critically, jostling with the French in the Illinois country south of the Great Lakes, and on the Upper Mississippi. For all that they traded with them, it had long been evident to the Indians that the American English were colonisers, threatening the hunting grounds of the Mohawk, Allegheny and Ohio valleys from New York, Pennsylvania and Virginia, and their resistance to this expansion was hardening; in this they were already finding allies in the French, who were determined to halt the English progress by the occupation of the Upper Ohio Valley. The struggle for the control of the interior, with the Virginians in particular determined to fight for their claims, was imminent [**doc. 12**].

The economy of the Thirteen Colonies was diversified by geography. In the south, Maryland and Virginia lived chiefly on the export of tobacco; and while North Carolina produced some, naval stores were its main contribution to the wealth of the Empire. In South Carolina the staple crops were rice and indigo; Georgia was regarded as little more than a strategic counterweight to the potential threat of the Spanish in Florida. Quite clearly, the southern colonies fitted well into a mercantile economy which valued such commodities so highly; but while they dutifully accepted British manufactures in exchange, their relations with the mother country were not without difficulty. Their planters were often in debt to English merchants, and in their need to repay were sometimes led into an overproduction which brought falling prices; then, and especially in Virginia, they sought westward expansion in order to add to the land they had exhausted. The middle colonies were also by 1750 the source of some disquiet; for while the industrial potential of New York was not realised, the iron industry of Pennsylvania was developing rapidly and looking for an increasing share of the imperial market for small-scale metal goods.

It was in New England, however, that this growing tendency of the colonists to compete with, rather than complement the economy of Great Britain, was becoming most marked. Save for the famous white pine of New Hampshire, the traditional source of the masts of the Royal Navy, it offered little that was acceptable in the current scale of mercantile values; yet the need for British manufactures in these most sophisticated parts of the American Empire was the more urgent. They paid for them by shipbuilding and shipping, supplying the craft and maritime services which had made Boston the most important seaport of the empire outside the British Isles; by the export of lumber, fish, flour and agricultural produce to the West Indies; and by a considerable share, held chiefly by Rhode Island, in the Atlantic slave trade. The profits from these activities, however, often in the form of bonds drawn on London, were insufficient to sustain a rising standard of living, and they had extended their trade, quite illegally, into the French West Indies. From them, by 1750, came a good proportion of the molasses that had become essential to one of the most flourishing industries of

New England: the distilling of rum, centred mainly on the refineries of Boston and Rhode Island. Its profits brought furs and slaves to be re-sold, paid for British manufactures, and enabled the northern colonies to buy the raw materials on which it rested and so allow the process to begin all over again. Thus New England sat uneasily in the framework of the mercantilist empire; and while before 1756 the British authorities did little about their illegal commerce, partly because it drew valuable bullion from France and Spain and partly because it enabled the New Englanders to buy more British manufactured goods, the economy of the northern colonies would be the most susceptible to any attempt to enforce the laws of trade as they existed on paper, and to impose any new forms of taxation (**40**). They would suffer particularly from the rejection of the opportunity that would be offered in 1763 to extend British power into the French islands and thus turn an illicit trade into a perfectly proper one.

The laws of trade which in theory governed the economic development of the overseas empire had as their object that of making it self-sufficient and ready, if necessary, to wage successful war against European rivals whose power rested upon similar systems; it was also designed to reconcile the frequent commercial conflicts between its parts, and of these the resentment felt by the sugar interests of the British West Indies at the illicit trade between the New England colonies and the French and Spanish islands is an excellent example.

By a series of Navigation Laws, from 1660 on, the monopoly of the intercolonial carrying trade was reserved for the ships of Britain and her colonies, securing a ready supply of craft and seamen. Supporting them was a series of Acts which forbade the colonies to sell certain staple products directly to other countries; these included, from 1660, sugar, tobacco, raw cotton and indigo, and, in the early years of the eighteenth century, rice, molasses, rum, naval stores and furs were added to what were known as the enumerated commodities. This regulation of colonial economic life was completed by the protection of a growing British industry; indeed, the rapid evolution of the factory system came to be one of its main results, for this vast influx of raw materials brought a great imbalance of commerce which could only be redressed by industrial growth. The total effect was to free Britain from reliance on foreign sources of raw materials, giving her the first claim on her own areas of supply and the power to deny them to her competitors; if, on the other hand, the produce of empire did go to foreign ports, Britain was enabled to lay customs duties on them and share in the profit made by their re-export.

The advantages to Britain were clear; it was more difficult then, and little easier now, to strike a balance between these and the benefits gained by the colonies themselves. The southern planters were assured of a vital English market for their commodities, and some recent American writers have suggested that behind this 'most important cement of empire' vital shipping and shipbuilding interests were allowed to grow unharmed; certainly in 1775 one-third of all the shipping in the empire was built in New England (26,28). The Navigation Laws were not mischievously designed, and the system they upheld was far less oppressive than those of France and Spain (32). It did try to mediate fairly between the competing claims of the British overseas possessions; it suppressed a flourishing tobacco-growing project in Britain, and when the West India interest formally protested that the New Englanders' traffic in French molasses was depriving them of a valuable export trade and assisting French planters in their attempt to drive British sugar from the European market, even to the point of French sugar, after refining in New England, being passed off as British in the home market, the Molasses Act of 1753 put a prohibitive duty of sixpence per gallon on all imports of foreign sugar, rum and molasses into British territories. That it was only slackly enforced, through the acquiescence of the home government and the wholesale bribery of customs officers, lends force to the suggestion that surveillance of the system was not strong, and that as a consequence the colonists were in a far from impoverished condition on the eve of the French wars. Burdens were light, and there is evidence of adequate capital for expansion; certainly the rapid and remarkable growth of population that was to provide one of the essential social factors in the story of the American Revolution had begun. While all this may not be the direct result of the mercantile system, there is little evidence that such growth was being inhibited by it, and none at all that the Americans ever called into question the right of the home government to regulate commerce (28). Where, in fact, the system hurt, it was evaded, and when the Revolution came, its origin can hardly be called mercantile. Even in the widespread resentment at its tighter regulation after 1763 there are few protests about mercantilism as such. The hatred of those years was of its enforcement, and of those who enforced; not of an old colonialism revived, but of a new imperialism which had its roots in an expression of parliamentary authority and which groped clumsily towards a new conception of imperial organisation. In practice it would rise but little above that unimaginative mercantilism which Adam Smith stigmatised as 'the sneaking arts of underling tradesmen' (41). The reasons for the American rejection of British policy after 1763 are to be found less in their fear of a revival of the old colonial system than in their resentment of the manner of its renewal, in a series of measures which threatened to halt the growth of the political independence which had grown up in the early years of the eighteenth-century, when, in the period of colonial neglect, they had won virtual self-government.

THE HABIT OF SELF-GOVERNMENT

In the colonies, representative government had been long established. In the Charter Colonies of Rhode Island and Connecticut it was deeply ingrained, with governors, officials and members of the Council all properly elected and of little accountability to the Crown. The proprietary colonies, Pennsylvania with Delaware, and Maryland, also had forms of representative government which rested on charters – those granted to the proprietors by the Crown and those subsequently issued by the proprietors themselves. The government of those remaining, the royal colonies, was based, with slight variations in Massachusetts, on the commissions and royal instructions granted to the governor at the time of their foundation; but his responsibility for the administration, where he also held full naval and military powers, had more and more become limited by the growing pretensions of the provincial assemblies.

While the councils of each colony were generally chosen by the governor himself from its more prominent citizens, and while he possessed the royal powers of dissolution and prorogation, and used them more frequently than in England, the elected assemblies were by the middle of the eighteenth century making widespread claims to share many of the privileges of the House of Commons itself. By then two vital rights had been generally conceded, those of giving assent to laws and taxes, and of initiating legislation; and while it was one of the assumptions of the old colonial system that each province should provide funds for its own administration, to be used by the governor at his discretion, the consistent refusal of most colonial assemblies to provide a permanent civil list made it possible for them to place serious limitations on his executive powers over the direction of policy and the appointment of officials. The coming of war in 1756, and the need to win the loyalty of the colonists, helped to establish a parliamentary practice which approached very closely to that of Great Britain (**33,34, 35**).

The issue of whether these colonial assemblies could go further and effectively challenge the authority of Parliament itself, would be the central one of the American Revolution. Governors had never been less than fully aware that all colonial legislation should conform not only with the charter of the colony in question, but with the laws of Great Britain; and in 1696 Parliament had decided that any measure passed by a colonial assembly which was repugnant to British law, or to any future statute that might be applied to the colonies, should be made void. At the same time, in the course of the eighteenth century, governors had reserved the matter of assent to certain bills to the Crown, and were given close theoretical instructions about their own rights in this respect. While, therefore, in practice imperial authority had weakened, these statutory limitations remained and would be reasserted. For the mood of British policy, in spite of all that had happened, could move easily from the acquiescence of the period before the Seven Years War to a hardening after it, when growing world responsibilities would lead ministers to insist that the strength of the empire as a whole could only be properly and adequately husbanded by the legislature at the centre; while the tendency of the colonies at this time to look inwards and westwards would reinforce the official view that in the context of this wider empire they were of such limited vision as to make their assemblies no more than subordinate corporations [doc. 10]. As the detailed policies which flowed from this general view were applied, colonial leaders would resist them, for their legislatures were in their eyes much more than local bodies which depended on the favour of the British government for their existence; they were parliaments which possessed in their own spheres as much validity as that at home. The dispute would be the more bitter in that it occurred within a family with a common political inheritance, where an overlapping constitutional experience brought every chance of similar disputes over matters of interpretation (45).

But while constitutional issues were vital, it would be wrong to see the American Revolution as in essence a democratic movement. Those who pressed their legal and constitutional claims in much the same terms as those used by Englishmen had reproduced in the New World many of the social features of the home country; they belonged for the most part to a distinct ruling class composed of landowners, merchants, lawyers and office-holders, roughly marked off from a middle class which, although it generally shared the franchise with them, was professional rather than landowning or mercantile. Beneath was a propertyless labouring class, and a whole breed of frontiersmen who were coming to resent the control of a privileged tidewater whose interests were not theirs and whose background was almost entirely European. Their way of life, like their religion, was primitive, and they were often too little represented and too heavily taxed, as the Regulator Movement would show **(1)**; thus, beneath the constitutional conflict with the British there was a political and social conflict within the colonies themselves that was to have a significant effect upon it. For while what is loosely called public opinion on such issues as taxation, quartering and military excesses was not difficult to rouse, and could the more easily be sustained by a more vital tradition of public controversy built on the radical press and the direct democracy of the Town Meeting, the problem for those who sought to make use of it, whether deliberately or not, was whether it could be sufficiently controlled to allow them to redefine their relationship with Britain without the complication of a social upheaval inside the colonies [**doc. 16**] .

THE ANGLO-AMERICAN COMMUNITY

It was in a broader context, however, that social change was most important. The rate of population growth and of westward settlement increased rapidly after 1750. From then until 1775 the population of the Thirteen Colonies doubled, as did the value of the goods they exported to England — reaching nearly £2 million on the eve of the Revolutionary War — to Europe and the West Indies. The colonies were coming to occupy a highly important place in the strategy of the empire and the economy of the world at the very moment when they were on the way to the discovery that their ties with the mother country rested on a constitutional relationship that could be defined only with considerable difficulty, and a set of economic regulations that were seldom applied and consistently ignored. Equally vital, yet often forgotten, is the fact that at this critical point in their development there was little that bound them to each other.

In these changing conditions, most marked in the third quarter of the eighteenth century, this unsatisfactory relationship with Britain, with the world, and with each other, could not endure. It is a truism that the natural social and economic growth of the colonies over the years had made it difficult for them to remain within a mercantile empire of the traditional sort. This, however, is to look at the question largely from their point of view, and it is perhaps more relevant to suggest that their rapid growth brought them into such essential contact with the issues of power politics and economic strength which so concerned the British as the eighteenth century went on, as they struggled to sustain a growing world responsibility, that the Parliament at Westminster was bound to try to create a new imperial organisation in which the American colonies were cast to play a vital role; they were in truth becoming too important to remain outside it **(40)**. The men who conducted British affairs, however, even if they had fitful glimpses of future empire, were only able to seek to create it in terms of present sovereignty, so that it would seem little more than the recreation of past ties which had been neglected. They tried to impose their own view of what the future relationship between Britain and her dependencies should be; the American colonists refused to accept it, and, in setting out an alternative, began the journey towards independence that would take them into an association with each other, built on a conception of shared sovereignty that had eluded the British.

A brief glimpse of the problem that was to be so important later may be seen as early as 1754. At the prompting of the British Government, a conference of the representatives of those colonies most affected by the growth of French power after 1750 met at Albany. The colonial disunity that the British were to discern much more clearly in the major war that was to follow was all too apparent; New Jersey, with no frontier at risk, would not take part, while the Virginians were negotiating separately with the Indian tribes of the Ohio Valley. Yet the delegates present, under the guidance of Benjamin Franklin, produced a plan imaginative enough to suggest the outlines of a future solution, even if, for this reason, it stood little chance of acceptance by the home government [doc. 1]. They proposed the setting up of a new intercolonial organisation, with a President-General appointed by the Crown and a Grand Council elected by the separate colonies, to formulate policies for Indian affairs and the settlement and defence of the western lands, and with sufficient authority over internal taxation to sustain them. These representatives thus looked forward to the Galloway Plan of 1774, and to the years when more imaginative minds on both sides of the Atlantic would seek a freer colonial relationship; while the suggestion that the policy for the west and the raising of a revenue to support it could be left largely in American hands was to be an essential element in the Shelburne proposals of 1768. But if the Albany Plan was resisted by the mercantilist thinking which dominated British policy, so also was it uncongenial to a colonial mood that was still strongly separatist. Both sides would have to go far, and through war, before they could begin to understand the demands of the new forms of political association, whether commonwealth or federal, which they would develop in the nineteenth century.

THE SEVEN YEARS WAR

The war with the French which came officially in 1756 and ended in 1763 brought the empire to the point of crisis. There was, of course, considerable resentment in Britain at what was considered to be a wholesale evasion by the colonists of their mercantile responsibilities and at their not unfriendly attitude to the Bourbon powers. At the same time there was a much more significant awareness that the system of which the colonies were but a part had failed; it had not produced an imperial organisation ready to sustain a long war, and it was, after it, costing far more to operate than it yielded. Of most immediate import-ance, however, was that at the end of it the French empire in North America had gone for ever, lessening the dependence of the Thirteen Colonies on Britain, and at the same time making it unnecessary for successive home governments to wink at the sort of constitutional con-cessions which had made it easier for them to retain their allegiance. But most vital of all, against the background of this less artificial rela-tionship, was that the questions which had led Britain into war with France would now bring her into serious conflict with her own colonies. The western lands, the defence of the frontier, the preservation of the Indian hunting grounds: these would become the issues that would be-gin the disruption of the Anglo-American community, and they would all be deeply affected by the crucial decision at the end of the war to retain Canada and the western lands at the expense of the wealthy sugar producing island of Guadeloupe.

The arguments for keeping Guadeloupe provide an excellent illustra-tion of mercantilism, for the extension of British power into the French West Indies would have considerably weakened the Bourbon naval pres-ence in the Caribbean, produced more sugar for the commodity market, and sanctioned and extended the already powerful New England trade relations with the foreign islands, giving them an increase in revenue that would have deterred them from becoming serious manufacturing rivals to the British. The arguments of those who wished to retain the French mainland territories were more imaginative. Franklin and his venturesome friends looked to some form of the partnership in coloni-sation with Britain that had collapsed at Albany in 1754, and they were supported by those in England who believed that a controlled westward expansion would also serve the purpose of postponing American indus-trialisation. Some, like Pitt, determined to see that Wolfe had not died in vain, caught a glimpse of the territorial empire of the future, and Choiseul was anxious to retain the French sugar islands. Thus Canada was chosen, instead of a policy which would have gone far towards meeting the problem of the Thirteen Colonies 'strategically by leaving the French at their backs and, commercially, by providing them with a large legitimate vent in the West Indies' (25). It was a decision of enor-mous importance. If the capture of Quebec began the history of the

United States, it was mainly because it set for English administrations a novel problem of imperial government, in which they were required to define a new frontier in a wilderness peopled by primitive tribes and settle at the same time the much more difficult issue of who was to pay for its defence. The extent of their dilemma, however, can only be understood when it is realised that this was not the only frontier of the empire. Britain in 1763 had reached the threshold of an imperial power in both west and east which, while it would give her the key to world domination in the nineteenth century, would also demand in its administration a high degree of understanding and imagination.

THE CONSTITUTIONAL DIVIDE

Her political experience rested on a simple and insular conception of parliamentary government; it had not, by 1763, given her the vision to see her colonial possessions in any other category but that of dependent states. The new imperial organisation could only be achieved, therefore, by an expression of the will of the British Parliament, and while its broad aim would remain the pursuit of economic greatness and world power, the essential problem of finding a sound constitutional relationship that would allow the Americans to remain inside it, and contribute to it, was never widely understood. As the political leaders on both sides groped towards it, lessons were learned that would be of vital importance to those who would construct the freer associations of the nineteenth century; the failure to do so in the eighteenth century was, paradoxically, brought about by an inability to bridge the gulf between different interpretations of political ideas once held in common (6).

The vital common belief was that of opposition to any form of arbitrary government (53). In the seventeenth century in England it had been represented by the executive power or, more loosely, the monarchy; and the struggle waged against it by the forces of Parliament had turned chiefly on the claim of men not to be taxed without their consent and their right to resist all manifestations of tyranny, whether it involved the curtailment of the powers of the assembly in which that consent was expressed, the use of prerogative courts in which trial by jury was suspended and the judges were not sufficiently independent of the king, interference with religious liberties, or the threat posed by a large standing army. The conflict had been pushed to its limits in civil war and vindicated by the great constitutional settlements of 1688 and 1701. The actions of those who sought to defend these rights were sustained by a political philosophy in which the most frequent appeals were to John Locke, who claimed broadly that rulers held their power in trust to provide government that was beneficial, and that it could be withheld from them if they transgressed upon this contract made between them and their people; and to an even earlier tradition by which the rights of Englishmen were held to be rooted in the common law, which, for some, encompassed a natural or God-given law [doc. 11a].

Those who used such ideas to enlarge their share of political and economic power in the seventeenth century came predominantly from the wealthy and influential landed and mercantile classes. Secured in the eighteenth century by the constitutional victories thus won, and reinforced by a grip on an imperfect territorial electoral system that they were able to turn to their own advantage, their successors were not disposed to place fresh limitations on the power of a governing machine which they now so effectively controlled. The unlimited sovereignty of what could now be termed the King-in-Parliament became the vital doctrine of these years, and the statute law that was built on its enactments, rather than the older common law, became the mainspring of the Constitution. Blackstone's views of its supreme power, expressed in the *Commentaries* of 1765, became the favoured ones of the age, and Locke's theory of contract was regarded as little more than theoretical conjecture [doc. 3]. It could hardly be seriously disputed – and this rested also on the Statute of 1696, which insisted that the legislation of the American assemblies should conform to the will of Parliament – that this supreme power applied to the colonies as well.

When the colonies resisted the policies of British governments after 1763 they would do so in terms of the constitutional battles of a hundred years before. It has been aptly suggested that the dissident immigration which made New England skimmed the milk of bitterness from Britain, and ensured that its final struggle with authority would take place at another time and in another continent (41). The legislatures of the colonies had in general by 1763 used their financial powers so as to gain a bigger share in government; and in their efforts to retain it and extend it they would collide headlong with an executive of governors, judges and officials who were heavily identified with the postwar policies of the British Government. But the authority on which these rested was far more powerful than the shallow-rooted tyranny of the Stuarts. It was with the might of an Imperial Parliament absolutely confident in its own limitless power that the colonists would have to contend, one which saw colonial organisation in terms of general subordination and which held the provincial assemblies to be of no more account than the English corporations. It was a mood utterly different from that in which its predecessors had set out to curb the executive power of kings and royal servants in the seventeenth century.

When the colonial leaders set out their case in this spirit they found little response, in spite of the fact that the issues of the quarrel should have been familiar to all Englishmen. For the Americans were good Whigs of an earlier sort. They assumed, simply, that government was set up in order to promote the public welfare, whether at home or in the colonies, and they would say so very clearly in the Declaration of Independence. If this implied contract were to be broken and the trust betrayed, then those who suffered were obliged to reclaim the political authority they had surrendered. The right of resistance was still to them an essential part of the English political tradition, and it would be justified as earlier Englishmen had justified it, for acquiescence in arbitrary government would encourage rulers to establish permanent forms of tyranny. Thus it would be possible for the true Whigs in England, who condemned what they believed to be the paralysis and corruption of their political life, to give support to the American cause [doc. 11a].

Yet the path for most Americans would not be an extreme one. The English Whig of the seventeenth century had looked in the main for the reconstitution of a stable and ordered society which tyranny had distorted, and in which obedience to good law was every bit as important as resistance to bad (53). Rebellion in the colonies would only come, as it had come in England, when the fear of enslavement had become widespread, when all other means of averting it had been tried, and after frequent appeals to representative bodies of public opinion — for the American leaders would petition regularly and act finally only after the holding of a series of congresses [docs 8,21]. If caution was to be the distinguishing feature of the long prelude to war, it was not only because of the fear of social and political tensions within the colonies that might disturb the balance of power. The fear of the accusation of illegality haunted good Whigs; but if in achieving their ends they were forced to make frequent appeals to mass opinion, they would, like all those who begin revolution, have difficulty in holding to an even and moderate course.

For ideology bred an extremism of its own, one that had little to do with political or social ambition. It came to a marked degree from an awareness among American leaders of their special place in the evolution of a new political order, and a conviction that the path already taken towards it before the middle of the eighteenth century could not arbitrarily be reversed, and would lead to a destiny of the sort discerned by John Adams in 1765. 'America was designed by providence for the theatre on which man was to make his true figure, on which science, virtue, liberty, happiness and glory were to exist in peace' (56). The dispute with the British was but one stage of a long process which would go on into the period of the building of the state and federal constitutions, but it occupied the years that were the most vital in the making of the new nation, in which its growing conviction of a brilliant future came to rest upon a dramatic interpretation of its past.

The origins of American pre-revolutionary thought, as Bernard Bailyn has shown, are mixed ones (45). It was full of appeals to the classical past; it was indebted to the Enlightenment, and to the belief that men possessed natural rights which it was the duty of governments to foster – glimpsed in passages from James Otis and clearly developed in the Declaration of Independence; it was steeped in the traditions of the English common law and of individual freedom, which the parliamentary statutes of the period after 1763 seemed to threaten; and there were clear threads of that New England Puritanism which helped to sustain the growing conviction that the Americans had been in some way divinely chosen to cleanse the world of tyranny and corruption. It was distinguished most, however, by its identification with the stream of English political radicalism which cherished in the first half of the eighteenth century the purer Whig traditions of the seventeenth, preaching the validity of natural and contractual rights, and the virtues of an idealised constitution which preserved liberty by reason of the balance existing between its three parts: executive, legislature and judiciary. These English radicals, however, like Hoadly and Molesworth, believed that political and individual liberty was now less in danger from the first as from the pretensions of the second, and even that both had now merged in corrupt and sinister partnership. In the hands of men like Walpole and Newcastle, Whig ideas had become institutionalised, frozen into a method of government, and its exponents were undermining the parliamentary virtues as insidiously as any Stuart king (45).

The standing of these writers in England was small, for an age of transition and political instability in which the traditions of workable responsible government had not been secured, and the royal will could no longer sustain administration by itself, called for the skill and management of those who understood that in such conditions influence was the vital cement of government (11). But from the distance that was so vital to the American question, and in colonies where there was a broad electorate and a tradition of direct and active democracy, and where colonial executives could still be seen as agents of English tyranny, the prevailing practices of English politics were seen in simpler and more sinister terms. The writings of the 'pure' Whig critics of Walpole and Newcastle became vital ingredients in revolutionary thought, and it is not surprising that the Americans were, in Burke's brilliant phrase, ready to 'snuff tyranny in every tainted breeze', and to believe that the power which had been wrested from the Stuarts and handed in trust to the representatives of the community as a whole, was once more about to be pushed beyond its legal limits. The victory of 1688 had been squandered in Britain; it could be preserved in America only with the utmost vigilance.

Distance is once more vital. The modification of the power of the Whig oligarchy inside Britain was achieved with little upheaval because the rising middle class which challenged it was able to come to terms with the social and political assumptions upon which it was built, joining the wealth of industry to that of land and adapting an existing machinery of government. But power exercised, even if in shared constitutional terms, on behalf of communities that were three thousand miles away, and with social and economic backgrounds that were not only different but antagonistic, would lead to disputes that could only be resolved through the evolution of a much looser constitutional relationship. For in view of the social and economic momentum within American society at mid-century, and of the growing awareness of its leaders that they could work out a destiny for themselves in a new and exciting continent whose problems were barely understood by the statesmen at home, and go on to build a freer and less corrupt form of government, it is hardly to be expected that they could be contained within a revived form of an old relationship [docs 23,24). The full realisation of this would take time; thus the young John Dickinson, in London in the election year of 1754, was appalled by the political corruption so rife around him; yet he was also aware that here were the sources of the legal and constitutional traditions of his own country.

PART TWO

Development

3 The First Crisis

THE GRENVILLE PROGRAMME: IMPERIAL REORGANISATION

While it is far from easy to weigh accurately each of the factors that went into the making of British policy after 1763, it is even more difficult to discern a deliberate policy of tyranny of the sort so feared by the Americans. For it is not easy to discern a consistent ministerial policy of any sort (15,16). Administrations were not built on the solid and legislatively fruitful foundations of the single-party majority; they were broadbased, they existed on consensus, and their political support was constantly at risk. The most that can be said is that in the twenty years after the Peace of Paris that consensus was in favour of a firm policy towards the Americans, and that those who possessed moderate and helpful views on the imperial question did not find it easy to get a hearing. They might, like Burke and the Rockinghams, find it hard to express precisely how the sovereignty that they at heart believed in should be qualified; or, like Shelburne, find personal failings getting in the way of sound political views; or like Pitt, pursuing a policy of political isolation, make it difficult for men of enlightened views to come together (17). It was considerably easier for those with orthodox views, like Grenville and Townshend, to impose them on the conduct of affairs.

There were two broad reasons for this. The first was in the general attitude of the politicians of the day. The mood of the English country gentleman who dominated the House of Commons was essentially conservative and patriotic. He identified American patriotism with English radicalism, and was easily persuaded that the low level of his land tax depended on the vigour with which the colonial revenues were collected. He was also in broad agreement with the groups which made up the Grenville administration that the principles of 1688 meant above all that the supremacy of Parliament should be affirmed, and used to pursue a colonial policy which would salvage the fortunes of his country. The second is to be found in the instability of ministerial government in the decade after 1760, for shortlived and uncertain administrations gave the permanent officials a considerable influence upon affairs. These men were spread over the several departments that became concerned in the American question, but the main stream of their advice came, through the Privy Council and the Secretary of State for the Southern Department, from the permanent officials of the Board of Trade and Plantations [doc. 13]. They initiated a good deal of the American legislation of the day; their thinking always reflected mercantile ideas; and they favoured in general policies of coercion and the assertion of British rights. They played a large part in the attempt to create a centralised empire after 1763, adding in detail the vital administrative machinery that would make effective the claims of Parliament to a sovereign authority over the colonies.

The Grenville programme so built was comprehensive, and it falls into two broad areas: the regulation of the frontier and the western lands, and the ways in which the funds for this policy were to be raised; whether or not English statesmen had decided on a deliberate attempt to destroy American liberties, they were painfully aware of a National Debt which had risen from £55 million in 1756 to over £130 million in 1763, and of an acute domestic financial problem. Thus, with new and demanding world responsibilities which were not confined to America alone, in which the cost of garrisons was estimated to be running at some £400,000 annually, with a crisis in home finance, and with little evidence of any willingness in America to search for a continental solution, the power of the Imperial Parliament was invoked (4).

The Proclamation of 1763, which derived in part from previous administrations, was the result of a perennial concern over the safety of the Indian hunting grounds and the future of the fur trade, and sharpened by the intercolonial quarrels which were beginning to break out over the interior; and it was brought into being immediately by the Pontiac Rising of 1763, at root an expression of Indian unease at the removal of French power and the consequences of American penetration, and during which the apparent unwillingness of even those colonies most closely threatened by it to defend themselves adequately served to confirm the view of the home government that a more positive frontier policy would have to be enforced (30).

It was the work of the permanent officials rather than of Parliament, and its assumption was that the elimination of French influence had for a time at least removed the need for any permanent settlement of the west [doc. 2]. This would lead to the establishment of inland colonies that would be of little mercantile value and difficult to control; they would also limit the profits of the fur trade and provoke the Indian tribes by threatening their traditional hunting grounds. It established a temporary and approximate line along the watershed of the Alleghenies beyond which settlement and unlicensed trade would be forbidden, and it set up Commissioners of Indian affairs to supervise such trade as was to be allowed. Indian land was to be bought on behalf of the Crown and leased to private settlers in accordance with overall policy; but it was made clear that the wish of the British Government was that American colonisation should for the present go north into Nova Scotia and south into East and West Florida, and not into the interior.

The consequences of this first attempt at imperial organisation were momentous. For the decision was also taken that in French Canada the new province of Quebec should retain for the time being its old autocratic form of government, together with the Roman Catholic religion and French language, laws and customs. There was to be no apparent check on its expansion, and the seeds were thus planted of the fear of a Catholic despotism in the north, sanctioned and even fostered by the British Government itself, that was to make the Canadian issue such an important one in the development of the North American revolutionary crisis (25). At the same time, if this comprehensive policy was to be enforced adequately and purposefully from London by a revived imperial authority, money would have to be found both for the frontier garrisons and for the Indian Service. In the light of Britain's economic difficulties it seemed not unreasonable to Grenville and his colleagues that the Americans should make some contribution, and he sought to ensure this first, by a tighter enforcement of the existing Acts of Trade, and, second, by a measure to raise a direct revenue from the colonies themselves.

In the enforcement of the mercantile system, senior customs officials found themselves ordered to posts which had before been regarded as sinecures with instructions to apply the colonial regulations. Their powers were increased; they were offered half the proceeds from the sale of the illicit cargoes which they would thus be encouraged to seek out and condemn, and were given much more effective naval and military support. The Revenue Act of 1764 set up a Vice-Admiralty Court at Halifax, Nova Scotia, to try without benefit of jury those accused of smuggling, and it made customs officers immune from civil suits against them. The Plantation Act of 1764, which was to become more generally known as the Sugar Act, was the most comprehensive of the new laws. While it reduced the duty on imported foreign molasses to threepence per gallon, there was clearly every intention to collect it; it also placed a prohibitive duty on the entry of foreign refined sugar and banned entirely the importation of foreign rum.

In fairness to Grenville, these last two features indicate that the measure was also designed to strike some balance between the competing interests of the island planters, the New England colonists and the Treasury. It also contained a number of amendments designed to improve the working of the colonial system as a whole; while, for example, the list of enumerated commodities was lengthened, bounties were extended to the production of hemp and flax [doc. 5]. But for all this, and in the face of the evidence that the New England distilling industry could have borne without much trouble a much greater imposition, the Americans could not fail to discern a very real threat to their commerce (26). For whatever the economic burdens it produced, there is little doubt that the manner of its enforcement, with the changed attitude of customs officials, the provision of new courts, and the new regulations which accompanied it, was as obnoxious to the Americans as the Act itself. And so, though no more than the first cloud of the political storm that would burst later, was the preamble to the Act, clearly stating that it was designed for the purpose of raising revenue; this was something which had in the past been sharply distinguished from the general purpose of the mercantile system, that of the regulation of trade [docs. 4, 5].

Finally, in 1764, came a measure which helped to throw some of the colonial merchants into severe financial difficulties and to generate the heated atmosphere in which the resentment felt at all the other measures could smoulder into flame. The New England prohibition of 1751 was extended, and the issue of paper money as a legal means of exchange was banned in all the colonies; while its aim was to prevent the repayment of debts to English merchants in a depreciating paper currency, it served to show once more that the economic wellbeing of the colonies was not in their own hands, and it would take little more to make the leaders of colonial opinion demand full control over their own internal affairs.

It came with the Stamp Act of 1765. If, as it generally was, the preamble to the Sugar Act is ignored, the measure had done little more than extend a generally accepted method almost imperceptibly across the line which separated the regulation of trade from the collection of a revenue (40). The Stamp Act, in its attempt to raise an internal levy by direct taxation, constituted a novel use of Parliament's authority. Before, it had seemed to be no more than general and external, never reaching inside the boundaries of colonies which had gained a great deal of control over their own affairs; sovereignty was now to be applied specifically and internally. The measure was approved in the House of Commons by 205 votes to 49, and few could be found to challenge Grenville's assertions that the taxing power was a vital part of the sovereignty of the British Parliament over every part of its dominions and, in more understandable terms, that it was not unreasonable to ask the colonists to contribute £60,000 yearly to the defence of the British territories in North America. It was not a heavy imposition, but there seemed little chance that the colonies, together or alone, would provide anything like as much for their own defence [doc. 7].

To the Americans it seemed that Grenville was unwilling to consider any other alternative, although there is some evidence that he delayed the introduction of the measure in the hope that the colonists might be prepared to accept the obligation of taxing themselves (4). They saw an anxiety to centralise the revenues of the empire and to bring an end to the process by which royal governors had been forced to barter successive instalments of self-government in exchange for funds from their assemblies; and while, in these first stages of the struggle, the simple complaint would be raised by the Americans that they were going to be taxed by a parliament in which they were not represented, the issues went considerably deeper. Grenville was in fact seeking to give a new and tighter constitutional framework to an empire which had previously rested on acquiescence, raising difficult and fundamental questions about exactly where in this new imperial organisation sovereignty should lie, at the very moment when the Americans were experiencing a new oppression on the frontier and a greater interference with their commerce, and when some of them were in acute financial difficulties. Even if it could be claimed that the measure did not bear hardly on the Americans, the manner of its introduction was little short of inept; whatever its results, consultation between Britain and her colonies might have softened a blow whose provisions would affect the most significant and articulate members of American society, the lawyers, journalists and merchants who were the most able to point out the implications of a tax which had been imposed by Parliament without consultation, and which could be the precedent for an even harsher tyranny. The Grenville programme, beginning with the Proclamation of 1763 and crowned by the Stamp Act of 1765, contained the ingredients of a broadly sensible imperial policy which lacked only the one vital element: American consent (58).

RESISTANCE

The rejection of the Stamp Act was also a rejection of the authority of Parliament, of Blackstone's aggregate body of King, Lords and Commons whose actions 'no power can undo' [doc. 3]. This sovereignty had inevitably to include the right to tax, for, as stated in the simplest terms by the American Tory, Pownall, if Parliament 'have not that power over America, they have none, and then America is at once a kingdom of itself' (45). In attempting to reject, even to modify, such unqualified assertions of power, the Americans were led into a tangle of constitutional argument which in the end could be resolved only by complete separation.

Even before the crisis of 1765-66, the storm signals had gone up. In 1761 James Otis, writing on writs of assistance – the general warrants which the British had begun to use to counter wartime smuggling – had based his challenge on the fundamental law by which even Parliament itself was constrained, and had looked for its origins beyond the parliamentary victory of 1688 to the traditions of the English common law which enshrined it. Later, attacking the Sugar Act of 1764 and examining more closely than most Americans the preamble which would have assigned the new duties to the purposes of revenue, he claimed the existence of a higher, divine law which safeguarded the liberties of all those who lived in the British dominions, and their right of representation in all matters of taxation [doc. 4]. At this stage Otis believed that some form of American representation at Westminster would be enough, and that once this principle had been conceded, and the rights and liberties of the colonists guaranteed, there could be no question that a parliamentary body thus constituted was sovereign. But if it was not conceded, then an attempt would naturally be made to restrict the power of a Parliament in which the Americans took no part; and the attempt to distinguish between what the Imperial Parliament could and could not do would inevitably lead to the position taken up by the more advanced thinkers of the 1770s, like John Adams in the *Novanglus Papers*, who proceeded from a demonstration of the sheer unfeasibility of American representation to a total denial of Parliament's competence to bind the Americans in their internal affairs [doc. 23]. For the moment, however, the vast majority of those who were first confronted by the issue in 1765, were not seeking dominion status. They saw no more than a simple and deliberate attack on their liberties as Englishmen, in which the administrations at home were abetted by local tyrants in the shape of unpopular governors and placemen, and sustained by the new Vice-Admiralty courts and the orders first sent out by the King in Council in 1761, forbidding the issue of judges' commissions on any other condition but that of 'the pleasure of the Crown'. These were the issues of a shared historical development, reflected also in the keen popular interest in the affairs of the English radical, John Wilkes. Such feelings were perhaps best expressed in 1765 by the Resolves of the Virginia assembly, moved by Patrick Henry, which stressed once more the right of all Englishmen in whatever part of the empire to representation before taxation, and concluded, logically, that only the General Assembly of Virginia could tax its inhabitants. The argument has been moved on from the position taken up by Otis in 1764, for there is here clearly no claim for representation at Westminster, merely the assertion of the taxing power of the colonial assemblies that would inevitably lead to a demand for a limitation of Parliamentary sovereignty (1). Between June and the end of 1765 resolutions of this nature were carried in the assemblies of Rhode Island, Pennsylvania, Maryland, Connecticut, Maine, South Carolina, New Jersey and New York. All were passed after full public discussion by the representatives of the people; all were strikingly and ominously similar; and there is little evidence in any of them that the Americans were in the mood to bear increased burdens of any sort, direct or indirect, internal or external; indeed, there are frequent complaints about the difficulties caused by the other Acts of trade (4). It should always be remembered that the debates of the colonial assemblies at this time were not untainted with demagoguery, and Henry was a rising and ambitious radical politician; but their resolutions as a whole are essentially and moderately summarised in the Declaration of the Stamp Act Congress of October, 1765 [doc. 8].

The gathering of nine of the thirteen colonies in New York is significant in itself in foreshadowing the closer union of the Americans that would be brought about by the continuing debate on British policy. Under the influence of John Dickinson, the Virginia Resolves were somewhat diluted; but while they stressed that the king's American subjects should render him allegiance, and give all the subordination to Parliament that was owed to it by his subjects in Britain itself, they also claimed the natural rights and liberties enjoyed by those subjects; and the firmness of the claim to be taxed only by their own assemblies reinforced the logic of the Virginia Resolves. There were also more general complaints about the extension of the practice of trial without jury and the powers of the Vice-Admiralty courts, the chronic lack of specie, and the harmful effects on American economic life of the recent measures for the regulation of trade.

Most interestingly, the delegates expressed their belief in the mutual benefits that would come from a proper relationship with Great Britain, with the rights and liberties of the colonists duly protected. The search for this link is at the heart of the debate on the American Revolution, and in a subsequent petition to the House of Commons at the end of 1765, drawn up by men remote from the heated atmosphere of competitive debate in the assemblies, a brave attempt was made to define it. A sound distinction might well be drawn, they suggested, 'between the necessary Exercise of Parliamentary Jurisdiction in general Acts, for the Amendment of the Common Law, and the Regulation of Trade and Commerce through the whole Empire, and the exercise of that Jurisdiction by imposing Taxes on the Colonies' (4). Even in their moderation, however, the delegates were seeking for a new statement of the imperial relationship in which the full sovereignty of the British Parliament was to be denied; and if the authority of the colonists to tax themselves was to be upheld, they would possess a measure of independence which could only grow with the passing years. They were asking to be allowed to define for themselves the nature of their subordination to Great Britain, and the fulfilment of the imperial reorganisation envisaged by Grenville would depend entirely on their good faith.

The distinction suggested by the petitioners stood little chance of acceptance after 1763. While it commended itself to many Americans because they believed that it summarised the terms of the old imperial relationship which had existed before 1750, and while it would be developed in a full understanding of all its implications to make the path towards the nineteenth-century Commonwealth relationship, it had little meaning for the British politicians who received it.

THE BRIDGE-BUILDERS

There were moderate men in 1765, however, who were anxious to develop the suggestion in the Petition that a distinction could be drawn between Parliament's right to regulate trade and its right to tax — between what, loosely and misleadingly, came to be distinguished as internal and external taxation — in the hope of constructing bridges between the two sides. Daniel Dulany, a Maryland lawyer, educated in England at Eton, Cambridge and the Middle Temple, and one of the most widely read of the opponents of parliamentary taxation, based his rejection of it on the simple and popular view that the colonists were not represented. Yet, and here it should be remembered that Dulany was a future Loyalist, he was prepared to concede that Britain's greatness as an independent power rested on her imperial position, and for this reason he accepted the right of the British Parliament to regulate trade. This was most commonly done by the imposition of external duties, and both these and the incidental revenue which came from them were quite permissible, since for him the essential difference between such duties and internal taxes was that the latter were intended 'for the single purpose of revenue' [doc. 9a]. This was a distinction, however, which, while it represented to many Americans a simple view of their past relationship with the mother country, contained a dangerous oversimplification, for there were few to warn, as Governor Hutchinson did in 1764, that external duties, efficiently collected, could drain the colonies of economic and political self-sufficiency just as effectively as any internal tax (45). Charles Townshend would render the distinction pointless.

The vain attempt to search for the line along which sovereignty could be divided was given more encouragement by the views held to have been put forward on this question by two of the most influential figures on either side of the Atlantic, both of whom occupied equivocal positions. In two speeches delivered on 14 January 1766, William Pitt took up the stand that he would hold until his death, and restated the older Whig values which reached back beyond the victory of 1688 and 'which placed the fundamental law of the constitution beyond parliament's reach'. For while he would have agreed with Blackstone that Parliament was 'sovereign and supreme in every circumstance of government whatsoever', this was not sufficient to allow it to alter the fundamental privileges of Englishmen which he held the Americans to share, and of these the most vital was that of representation before taxation.

Yet, in the imperial context, sovereignty without taxation could not exist, and the inability of the eighteenth-century mind to accept such a fundamental restriction of sovereignty may well have led to the general and wrong impression that Pitt went on to make firm distinction between internal and external taxation in his second speech of that day, and that in denying the first he had accepted the principle of the second. In truth, he rejected Parliament's right to tax the colonists in any form, for, like Dulany, he clearly stated that there was a plain distinction between impositions whose chief purpose was the raising of a revenue, whether internal or external, and duties imposed for the regulation of trade, even though the consequence of the latter might be an incidental revenue [doc. 9b].

To the misunderstandings of Pitt in this respect should be added the evasions of Benjamin Franklin when he was examined before the House of Commons a month later [doc. 9c]. It should be remembered that although Franklin had been in the colonies during the last months of 1765 and knew full well the American temper, his first intention as a colonial agent was to secure the repeal of the Stamp Act, and he shrewdly evaded the issue of whether his countrymen were denying the right of Parliament to tax them in general. It should also be borne in mind that the Rockingham Ministry, which had succeeded that of Grenville, was no less intent upon the repeal of the Stamp Act, and believed that their task would be easier if the impression was allowed to grow that the colonists would accept some form of imperial taxation. Thus they made little attempt to clarify Pitt's words, and encouraged Franklin to suggest that there was a valid distinction between internal and external taxation, mainly on the rather unconvincing grounds that the latter need not be paid, and that American thinking, while it might well reach that position in time, was not yet prepared to regard the two forms of taxation as one. It was thus possible, with two such formidable authorities to guide them, for moderates on both sides of the Atlantic to hold to a slender rope which Townshend would cut through.

An even frailer link between the two positions came with the attempt to justify the supremacy of Parliament by the assertion that the Americans were in fact indirectly represented in it. Its most typical expression appears in Soame Jenyns's *The Objections to the Taxation of our American Colonies, briefly considered* of 1765 [doc. 10]. His proposition was that since nineteen out of twenty Englishmen, particularly in the growing industrial areas, were taxed without being directly represented in the English Parliament, the Americans would do well to consider themselves virtually represented in an assembly in which the interests of all, voters and voteless, were safeguarded, and as the beneficiaries of a system in which they had in fact exaggerated the political rights which most Englishmen possessed. Pitt, in his January speeches, would have none of it, while Dulany countered the argument by maintaining that the true function of a representative assembly was the protection of its people from the oppression of government. In this most vital respect there was an important identity of interest between all Englishmen, whether enfranchised or not, since tyranny established at home would fall equally upon both. But that same interest need not exist between the people of Britain and the American colonists; the consequences of taxation, for example, might be vastly different, and levies which threatened the liberties of America might not be so damaging, and could even be beneficial, to the people of Britain. James Otis, who had asked for representation in 1761, was in 1765 quite sure that English members could not adequately represent American interests, and, reversing the argument, claimed that if virtual representation would not do for America, then so was it equally invalid for Britain.

There were, it seemed, representational imperfections on both sides of the Atlantic, as Pitt saw; and just as English Whigs believed that English liberties were at stake in America, so were leading American radicals intensely interested in the fate of Wilkes. Otis had seen what Dulany had resisted, that both Englishmen and Americans stood to lose much from the exertion of a common tyranny. Yet for all this, there were fundamental political differences which made the idea of virtual representation untenable. For if, in matters of sovereignty, the British Parliament had grown sufficiently in self-confidence to regard itself as supreme, so had it also become the embodiment of the nation rather than the merely representative assembly which reflected the separate interests of the groups which had elected it, a concept again that was to be expressed most accurately by Burke. The American experience was the reverse; they suspected the pretensions of central government, and their representatives, as delegates of the counties and townships which had sent them to the colonial capitals, stood for a local independence which had much more in common with the direct representation of the boroughs and shires of medieval England. This view would make it almost impossible for them to take in the niceties of virtual representation; and their determination to hold to it pushed them along the road to a more radical and direct form of democracy. Government, for them, could have no valid existence save in the will of the people to whom all representatives were directly accountable. Thus, once more out of impatience with an imperfect English parliamentary system came the strengthening of the view that it was the American mission to provide a purer version of the art of self-government.

REPEAL

Deeds, rather than words, exposed the shortcomings of the Stamp Act. An intercolonial agreement to import no British goods and honour no British debts until the Stamp Act had been repealed was followed by widespread rioting, and the intimidation of those who represented the authority of the administration. Men already designated as the collectors of the Stamp Tax were persuaded by one means or another to resign, and customs officers who at first refused to clear shipping without properly stamped documents were soon pushed into getting trade moving normally. The example of the Boston 'Sons of Liberty' was contagious; by early 1766 British authority hung by a thread, and there seems little doubt that it would have broken down completely had not news arrived in America of an impending change of policy. Grenville might well have brought on open rebellion in 1766 had not the king, for reasons quite unconnected with America, dismissed him and appointed the Rockingham administration.

While it is not easy to persist with the notion that the Rockingham group was the positive and consistent supporter of American rights (only one of the new cabinet, General Conway, actually voted against the Stamp Act) the new government saw the need for a Whiggish policy of concession (23). They were hopeful of gaining the support of Pitt, and knew full well the terms on which it would be given, and there seemed little point in going on with an assertion of authority which could not be sustained; but it is now more generally accepted that pressure from powerful commercial interests which were being harmed by the American boycott and the moratorium on debts, and on whose support in the Commons the administration to some extent depended, was the most compelling factor in repeal.

Yet for so many private members, and for at least one minister, Charles Yorke, the Attorney-General, the question of the American defiance of the legal powers of Parliament could not be evaded, however skilfully the administration manipulated petitions to the House that would emphasise the economic folly of the Stamp Act. Straightforward surrender was out of the question, and, to be fair to the Rockinghams, there is little evidence that they would have proposed it. Some favoured a modification of the Act, while others, convinced that only outright repeal would be sufficient, were searching for a formula that would leave the general supremacy of the Imperial Parliament intact. These divisions brought delay, but when Parliament reassembled in the New Year it was Pitt's speeches of January which crystallised the issue. Repeal was necessary because the Stamp Act had contravened the basic rights of both Englishmen and Americans; yet the sovereign authority of Parliament over America had to be asserted in 'as strong terms as can be devised' (3).

There were few to question what would happen to a sovereignty from which the power of taxation had been subtracted; and the leaders of the administration seemed most concerned that Pitt had apparently accepted the distinction of the Stamp Act Congress, that taxation was a matter for the colonial assemblies and the regulation of trade the concern of the British Parliament. The general belief that he had given his approval to external taxation obscured the issue and made the passage of repeal easier.

It would doubtless have been more difficult to achieve had not the Declaratory Act accompanied it; the Repeal found substantial opposition, but the assertion of right went through the Commons without a division and with only five votes against it in the Lords. The debate here, in February, is revealing, although it did nothing to resolve the substance of the argument over sovereignty (3). Lord Lyttleton gave a perfect illustration of the way in which Locke's views were being used to justify the supremacy of Parliament over what he called the 'inferior legislatures' of the colonies, and feared that a failure to sustain authority would have an unfortunate effect on the London mob. Camden, already a hero to the American radicals by having declared general warrants in the Wilkes case illegal, was virtually alone in his condemnation. He appealed to a Whiggism purer and older than that expressed by Lyttleton; the legislature was not wholly sovereign because it could not contravene the divine law, and if the Declaratory Act was to be construed as giving it the absolute authority to tax the Americans without their consent, that would be a power altogether too general. Lord Chancellor Northington took his stand on the consummation of parliamentary authority in 1688, and on the Act of 1696 which particularly extended that power to the colonies. Camden, returning to his theme, maintained that Locke's teachings had a universal validity: 'The supreme power cannot take from any man, any part of his property, without his own consent' [doc. 11a].

In fact, the general support for the Declaratory Act did not mean that there was any general agreement about its meaning. Pitt, and those who supported him, clearly believed that it did not sanction the right to tax. The Grenvillites, exposing the fundamental inconsistency in his argument, maintained that the concession that Parliament was unable to tax would be an admission that it was unable to legislate and that its sovereignty did not exist. The Rockingham group, including Burke, had little doubt that the authority they claimed for Parliament did include the taxing power — which did not make it any easier for them to work with Pitt — but believed that there should be a tacit agreement that it should not be used (20). Their belief in practical conciliation was illustrated by a number of small measures like the reduction of the molasses duty to one penny, an attempt to take some of the sting out of the colonial regulations.

The significance of the extreme claims that were made, however, is inescapable. Parliament, by its own act, had given itself a greater authority than had ever existed before. Its claim to tax the colonies had up to now rested on its role as the supreme legislature of the whole empire, and on the virtual representation of the colonies within it. Now this power was asserted simply because Parliament itself had declared that it had the right to do so. And while, in the general feeling of relief in America, there was a popular belief that Parliament had surrendered the right to tax, the more perceptive of the colonial leaders were aware that the Declaratory Act could make it more and not less overbearing, and that the conflict of sovereignties had merely been put off. Whether for reasons of joy or apprehension, most colonial legislatures reaffirmed their own competence in taxation and claimed that a great victory had been won; and the events of these months brought forward in colonial politics, especially in Virginia and Massachusetts, the men who were the most extreme supporters of colonial claims; and at the same time began the eclipse of those who had looked for a modest restatement of the colonial relationship (4). An embryonic unity had also been achieved, and a common sense of purpose was beginning to emerge.

The Grenvillites had been right in pointing out that the abandonment of their policies was a surrender to violence, even if they did not accept that they had helped to bring this about by failing to provide the means adequate to their enforcement. The colonists had made an Act of Parliament unworkable; they had put the policy for the frontier at grave risk; and they had demonstrated in fact that Britain could not tax them directly, and that therefore any debate like that of February 1766 about her theoretical right to do so was largely irrelevant **(40)**. And, it must be repeated, if the power to tax was in doubt, then so was the substance of any other sort of authority [**doc. 11b**]. The Grenvillites had seen, as the American patriot leaders would soon come to see, that this was at the heart of the problem. Pitt, apparently, could not see; while Burke, suggesting later that the compromise of 1766, with a right theoretically asserted and practically withheld, was the correct one and the point of true repose, did not stress enough that the American problem of the eighteenth century was like the Irish question of the nineteenth, a dynamic one, constantly moving forward, and that the keeping of that balance would depend on delicate and continuous adjustment. Some, including Burke and the Rockingham group, would be content not to press questions of financial and legislative authority in order to maintain it. Others would not, and chief among them was Charles Townshend.

4 The Gulf Widens

The Rockingham administration fell three months after the repeal of the Stamp Act. It was succeeded by a government headed by William Pitt, now Earl of Chatham, containing Camden and Conway, who had adopted liberal attitudes in the Stamp Act debates, and Shelburne, from beginning to end of the American question the almost consistent advocate of common sense and conciliation. But illness forced Chatham's virtual withdrawal in 1767; the administration lost cohesion, and the policies that might have been expected from it — a surrender of the right to tax and a vigorous reconstruction of the external imperial relationship — never appeared. Men like Camden found it difficult to give executive reality to the liberal sentiments of opposition. Shelburne was able to put forward a constructive and potentially useful plan for the settlement of the frontier question; but its effectiveness was nullified by new proposals of taxation put forward by Charles Townshend, the volatile and ambitious Chancellor of the Exchequer, who came to dominate the ministry and lead it towards a new American crisis (17).

SHELBURNE AND THE FRONTIER — THE ANGLO-AMERICAN COMMUNITY

It was by no means inappropriate that the Chatham ministry should have wanted to look closely at the frontier question, for its problems were the legacies of the war which Pitt had directed. The Indian problem remained, and with it the question of the fur trade and the proper disposition of the western lands. But for those of broader vision the frontier provided a deeper challenge that was bound up with issues of much wider importance: of Britain's relations with competing European powers, of how any new areas should be governed, related to the older colonies, and joined with them in a larger imperial organisation that might well have formed the basis for a renewed Anglo-American community. This, rather than the setting off of the immediate crisis over taxation, is the vital influence of the frontier on the course of the American Revolution and on the making of the new nation; for if the colonists would not accept the part reserved for them by Britain in the development of the North American continent, and within the framework of a new empire, then they would, in seeking for their own solution, find themselves driven into an independent continental union.

A sign of the broader imperial perspective came with the decision to renounce Guadeloupe, for all that it fitted the old mercantilist requirements, and take up the challenge of the west. The Proclamation of 1763 had sought to buy the time in which a coherent policy for the frontier could be worked out, and a good Indian Service under Johnson and Stuart was set up to enforce its proposals. But it began in practice, and after conferences with colonial governors and Indian chiefs, to allow a more reasonable and moderate line to become established west of the 1763 limits in the Upper Ohio Valley. At the same time, even beyond this, an unofficial and haphazard expansion went on, since it was impossible, after the failure of the Stamp Act, for the British authorities to forbid it completely, and some doubtless felt that if an outlet could be found for the expansive energy of the Americans it would dissuade them from manufacturing for themselves and provide further markets for British industrial goods; thus schemes like the Vandalia project (by which prominent Englishmen and Americans sought to buy and develop the area roughly corresponding to the modern region of West Virginia) even found semi-official patronage, while to others a blind eye was turned (25). There was little to attract the colonists to Nova Scotia and the Floridas; instead Yankees from New Hampshire and Massachusetts pushed into Vermont; from Pennsylvania, Virginia and Maryland, settlers found their way into the Ohio Valley; from Virginia again, and from North Carolina, they entered the Tennessee Valley. They quarrelled with each other as they went, and they brought fear to the Indians who had been taught to look to King George for protection [doc. 12]. By 1767 the problem of expansion had again become acute, and brought forward the Shelburne proposals of that year.

The enforcement of the policies of 1763 and 1764 would have required more troops at a time when the demand for lower taxation at home had become insistent, and when Anglo-American relations had reached a critical stage. Shelburne's plan was built on the belief that a controlled penetration of the west would, besides providing markets for British manufactures, make the Acts of Trade (which the Chatham ministry was determined to enforce) more acceptable to the Americans, and its roots were in the semi-official partnership between merchants and land speculators on both sides of the Atlantic. Richard Jackson, Member of Parliament and agent for Connecticut, was responsible for bringing Franklin, who was already deeply involved in the future of the Illinois Company, and Shelburne together, and thus to promote the partnership that was to bear fruit in the peace negotiations of 1782 (25). The essential proposals were for the creation of new inland colonies that would have extended the imperial boundaries in partnership with the Americans, with westward expansion guarded by British troops and forts, and eventually paid for by an anticipated income from quit-rents and land fees. In time the new colonies were to become responsible for Indian relations and stand on their own feet in all respects; but they would be indirectly compelled to cooperate with each other and with the British Government in the establishment of a new form of political organisation in North America which was a development of that suggested at Albany in 1754 [doc. 1].

The Shelburne proposals looked for a greater degree of colonial cooperation than in fact existed, but they broke chiefly on attitudes in which the limitations of British statesmanship were exposed. The Treasury, feeling towards retrenchment, was never likely to grant the initial funds that would be necessary for the setting up and development of the new colonies; neither was the ministry as a whole, after 1767, disposed to advance liberal policies in the interior while it was still struggling to maintain its authority on the seaboard. The greatest limitation of all, however, was in the mercantilism which still coloured the attitudes of the permanent officials, and it is nowhere better expressed than in the Report on the Shelburne proposals made by the Board of Trade and Plantations in 1768, and signed among others, by Soame Jenyns. It found no proof that westward expansion would put an effective brake on American industry, or that joint colonisation would promote closer imperial union; on the contrary, inland colonies would produce farming settlements which would foster the spirit of independence, and not the commodity-producing areas which should ideally have been near the seaboard and therefore accessible to British seapower. The success of the Shelburne plan was doubtful, and it would almost certainly have suffered the same fate as that devised at Albany, yet it showed more vision and imagination than could be found in the more limited minds of the Board of Trade [doc. 13]. It also foreshadowed the way in which the Americans themselves, without Britain, would approach the problem of the interior.

Yet discussion of the Shelburne proposals in this sense is academic, for while a policy of common benefit was being sought in the interior, Townshend had already gone far towards provoking a quarrel on the seaboard that would never be healed.

CHARLES TOWNSHEND AND JOHN DICKINSON

With complete lack of judgement, and with all the advantages of hindsight, Townshend revived the worst features of the Grenville policies so recently abandoned. In doing so, he thought little about Britain's world responsibilities, but followed the mood of a House of Commons which, anxious to see a reduction in domestic taxation and angry at the continued colonial defiance of the Mutiny Act of 1765 (which imposed the obligation of sheltering and feeding British troops), was ready to take up his suggestion that the Americans should be asked once more to contribute to their own defence. Thus he insisted on a withdrawal from the interior and the handing over to the colonies of the cost of the Indian Service, and in 1767 introduced the Revenue Act incorporating the notorious Townshend Duties and signifying the attempt to secure a revenue by taxes on external trade.

The value of these taxes to the Exchequer was by no means apparent, since of the articles Townshend chose to bear revenue charges only tea was imported in sufficient quantity to yield anything like a reasonable return; the rest – paints, glass, lead and paper – were not, and since the duty on them was likely to discourage the export of these British manufactures, the proposals made little sense even in terms of existing mercantile policy, while a more certain revenue might have been raised in Britain by retaining excises already paid and discontinuing drawbacks on exports. This confusion in policy betrayed the man and bewildered the Americans, and many of them believed that the real significance of the Townshend Duties must lie elsewhere. In this they were correct, for in three important respects they went significantly further than the Grenville proposals.

First they destroyed for ever the faint hope that the Americans might be content to distinguish between internal and external revenue, for Townshend rested his case on the rather devious testimony of Franklin to the House in the previous year and ignored the careful distinctions made by Dulany and Pitt and repeated in many colonial petitions, between a revenue which came incidentally from external taxation and one which was its main purpose [**doc. 9**]. Yet, second, they carried a threat which was absent from the Grenville proposals and pushed the dispute between Britain and her colonies towards constitutional deadlock. For Townshend wished to do more than merely use the revenues for the purposes of defence; he stated clearly in the preamble to the Act that he intended to turn them to the provision of something he had long advocated: a civil list in each colony which would make governors and royal officials independent of their assemblies and therefore much freer to carry out the imperial policies laid down in London [doc. 14]. This, for the colonists, was the crucial issue. They had already won considerable power over their executives through the control of supply, and it was in their eyes the most fundamental of the English rights and liberties which they claimed to share, and they had no intention of yielding up the ground they had won. Third were the associated measures which brought a similar reaction: the setting up of Vice-Admiralty courts at Boston, Philadelphia and Charleston, with their clear hint of the prerogative courts of the Stuarts, the new American Board of Customs at Boston, with wide powers, and the reduction of the powers of the New York assembly in order to force compliance with the terms of the Mutiny Act of 1765. The American patriot leaders, ever watchful of a conspiracy to destroy their liberties, saw the attack upon their constitutional freedom developing along a wide front.

Thus the political debate in America moved on to new ground, and was conducted by none more efficiently than John Dickinson, the retired lawyer from Pennsylvania, whose *Farmer's Letters* of 1767-68 were the most influential of all the pre-revolutionary pamphlets. Quietly, yet more persuasively than any writer before him, Dickinson accepted the opportunity to develop Whig ideas afforded by the Townshend duties. Like Chatham, he refused to distinguish between internal and external revenues and denied that Parliament had a right to impose either on people who were not represented in it. He saw instinctively the threat implied in the intention to create a civil list from the American taxation; it would enable British ministers to curb the colonists in any way they chose and, just as dangerously, set up repugnant military and ecclesiastical establishments [doc. 15].

Dickinson, however, was a constructive moderate, and from these two bases he went on to a discussion of the issue of sovereignty which came close to the heart of the whole problem. He saw that if its power of taxation was to be rejected and its pretensions to limit the competence of the colonial assemblies denied, then there was little left for the British Parliament to do in any future imperial organisation that would have any significant effect upon American life. Dickinson contended that the functions of the Imperial Parliament were quite separate from those of the legislatures of the constituent nations; they were simply to maintain the external bonds of empire and to regulate its commerce and economy, using for this purpose the revenues which came incidentally from them; while the Crown, in an anticipation of the part played by the Privy Council in the future Commonwealth, should sit in appeal 'from all judgements in the administration of justice' (45).

Sovereignty, in short, was to be divided. An overall body was to have a regulating but not a taxing power; this, together with control over their own domestic affairs, was to be left to the colonial legislatures. Yet while it was an essentially moderate proposal, by no means as extreme as the assertion already being heard that Parliament could not bind the colonies in any sense whatever, it met little response in Britain. The voice of Chatham was for the time still, and none of his colleagues who had before spoken with some understanding of the American cause seemed to possess the freedom in office to point out the constitutional dangers of the Townshend programme. Burke would later condemn it and produce a glimpse of the future Commonwealth remarkably similar to that outlined by the Pennsylvania farmer, but the Rockingham group was notably quiet (23). The possibility of conciliation built on the foundation of the distinctions and qualifications made by Chatham and Dickinson depended on moderate views gaining a hearing on both sides of the Atlantic; but the prevailing mood in Britain alone made it unlikely that the traditional concept of an undivided and undisputed sovereignty would easily be abandoned. It was restated forcibly and typically by William Knox, a Grenvillite, who, in a pamphlet entitled *The Controversy between Great Britain and her Colonies Reviewed,* published in London in 1769, rejected any of the attempts made by Dickinson and others to distinguish between what Parliament could and could not do in the imperial context. Its power was indivisible, and the bond between Britain and her colonies everlasting: 'All distinctions destroy this union; and if it can be shown in any particular to be dissolved, it must be so in all instances whatever.' Paradoxically, the sincere attempt by Dickinson to build purposefully a distinction between internal and external authority, and to find what moderate Americans would have regarded as an acceptable statement of imperial relations, had led to a hardening of attitudes. It is best illustrated on the British side by the appointment of the uncompromising Hillsborough as Third Secretary of State, with special responsibility for American affairs, in 1768 (58). The answering voice in America would also be an extreme one, and the moderate and legalistic arguments of Dickinson would find it hard to gain a hearing again.

RESISTANCE AND REPRESSION

The pattern of the opposition to the measures of 1767 was largely the same as in 1765. Resolutions in general support of Dickinson's views were passed by the provincial assemblies, and the first, from Massachusetts, was accompanied by a circular letter demanding common action. When Hillsborough denounced both, and after Governor Bernard had dissolved the Massachusetts Assembly for addressing a petition in similar terms to the king, others followed suit. Non-importation agreements covering almost the whole range of British goods were privately enforced by the merchants of Boston, New York, Philadelphia and Baltimore. In May 1769 Virginia's House of Burgesses adopted resolutions by George Washington which reaffirmed the sole right of the Virginians to tax themselves, and condemned the decision taken by the British Government earlier in the year to transfer radical agitators for trial in Britain. It too was dissolved for its pains, but, meeting on the following day as an illegal body, proclaimed an almost total embargo on British goods and set up the Virginia Association to enforce it. It was highly effective, and it was contagious; by the end of the year one colony after the other took up similar policies administered by extra-legal bodies of this sort. The pattern was ominous. As in 1765 the authority of the British Government had been flouted, but here for the first time were the faint signs of the power that was to take its place.

If peaceful petition and non-violent embargo owed a good deal to Dickinson's call for moderate action and to the difficulties of the American merchants, they derived also from a radical agitation that was political rather than economic, and which was reflected in the growing ascendancy in the popular politics of Boston of the radical lawyer, Samuel Adams. This had been the power behind the Massachusetts petition of 1768, and the months that followed saw the emergence of a highly organised agitation. For whatever reason, many Bostonians moved from embargo to a more positive resistance that made the customs service powerless, nullified the Vice-Admiralty Courts, and forced the newly created Board of Customs to move from Boston to the safety of Castle William and the protection of General Gage; among them were men of moderation who had rejected such methods in 1765, but who were now seeking and finding illicit access through the Dutch West Indies to the tea they could not do without. Once more it had become clear that the Acts of Trade rested upon consent and not compulsion; and the attempt to affirm a theoretical right to tax was being set aside. In this vain attempt to raise a few thousand pounds, valuable trade was being lost; and by the end of 1769 the fall of British imports in New York alone was over eighty per cent. The Revenue Act of 1767 had been a political blunder and an economic disaster, and the ministers in London had to retrieve the position Townshend had placed them in as best they could — for he had died in the same year. Conciliation, given the mood of the House of Commons, would not be easy, but neither were ministers ready for a policy of outright coercion; the troops in Boston were not used to enforce these disastrous policies, and when

Hillsborough moved to amend the charter of Massachusetts in 1769 George III was hostile and his colleagues lukewarm. Thus, the two coercive factors which were to do so much to bring on the final crisis were held back, and without them the only alternative for the ministry was a policy of non-provocation.

But it would carry no more conviction than that of 1766, and no minister of the Crown could have considered a change of direction without an acceptance of American subordination. This had always been the constitutional position even of Burke and the Rockinghams, and while in 1770, against a background of economic difficulty, the new prime minister, Lord North, abandoned the Townshend duties on the grounds that they made no mercantile sense, the levy on tea was retained in the spirit that Rockingham had passed the Declaratory Act, as a token of Parliament's right to tax in this way if it wished. Thus two measures now remained to poison Anglo-American relations, and to provide the legal basis for an assertion of authority which in the end would have to be sustained by force. For while the new ministry attempted small measures of conciliation by removing the quartering obligations from the Mutiny Act and partially ignoring the Vice-Admiralty Courts, the basic attitudes on either side remained unchanged. The Americans would not grant taxes to Parliament, and Parliament would not allow them to tax themselves; a workable relationship between them had not been found and a new pattern of empire had still to be created. The matters of Canada and the frontier had never been squarely faced, and the presence of the army, which in the end would have to enforce obedience, would become a powerful irritant. Beneath them all was the essential truth that the colonies needed the opportunity to grow: towards an independent economic identity, towards the interior, and, ultimately, towards self-government (40). If this was to be permitted by the British Government, there would have to be a difficult division of sovereignty. If Britain would not yield, then the empire would fall, for by 1773 the Americans had found enough momentum to enable them to go on to find a solution for themselves.

For the moment, with prosperity rising on both sides of the Atlantic, leading Americans seemed not too anxious to push their case too hard. Non-importation died out, with the Virginians the last to give it up in 1771; and while a discreet smuggling went on, the wealthier merchants seemed unwilling in general to support any more extreme actions for fear that they would strengthen the radicals. This was, in fact, the last chance for the sort of concessions from the king's ministers which might have driven a wedge between them; but there were none of the 'large constitutional gestures' that would have given validity to the moderates' position (41). Instead, irritating policies were persisted with or newly adopted, and greater strength was given to the radical cause.

Thus the serious currency problems in many of the colonies were ignored. The newly strengthened customs authority set out to collect its dues with purpose, and with provocation; and with the colonists determined to evade, harsh confrontations like that of the seizing and burning of the revenue cutter *Gaspée* off Rhode Island in 1772 were inevitable. The irritant already provided by the presence of British and mercenary troops was increased by Gage's decision to recall detachments from the frontier and place them along the seaboard. In this atmosphere events like the famous 'Boston Massacre' of 1770, when a detachment of redcoats in difficulties with a Boston mob fired into it and killed five people, were inevitable. Constitutional relations between the executive of governors and officials and their legislatures were made more bitter when the former implemented instructions from home to grant no more liberties. Nowhere were these relations worse than in Boston, where customs issues, the presence of the military and the memory of the 'Massacre', were contributing to a dangerous hardening of attitudes on both sides.

Here efforts to revive British authority took two rather more extreme forms. Governor Hutchinson convened the Massachusetts Assembly at Cambridge instead of Boston to remove it from the influence of the radical mob; while the home government decided to make the Governor's position stronger by paying his salary and those of the Massachusetts judiciary out of British funds, thus rendering them less dependent upon the assembly. The constitutional issue that was to destroy the old empire was seen most clearly in Massachusetts, and is nowhere expressed more precisely than in the exchange between the Governor and John Adams in 1772, when both sides disputed over the constitutional position. Hutchinson maintained that he knew of

no line that can be drawn between the supreme authority of parliament and the total independence of the colonies. It is impossible that there should be two independent legislatures in one and the same state, for although there may be but one head, the King, yet two legislative bodies will make two governments, as distinct as the Kingdoms of England and Scotland before the Union.

Adams was equally sure of the premise, but drew the opposite conclusion: 'If there be no such line, the consequence is, either that the colonies are the vassals of the parliament, or that they are totally independent'. Extreme assertions of authority were bound to bring extreme reactions.

The second followed from the first. If the statutory legislature was to find itself without power and, since it refused to meet at Cambridge, without existence, greater attention would inevitably be attracted to unofficial and more dangerous assemblies. The propagandist Sam Adams set out to turn the famous Boston Town Meeting into such a body; always, in local matters, a legitimate part of New England democracy, it now became widely renowned as an organ of radical resistance. Earlier it had used the emotion roused by the Boston Massacre to challenge the right 'of any exterior authority upon earth, to determine, limit or ascertain all or any of our constitutional or chartered, natural, or civil, political, or sacred, rights, liberties, privileges or immunities'; now in 1772 it brought issues which had been simmering for so long into the full light of day **(58)**. A 'List of Infringements and Violations of Rights' set out a catalogue of long-standing grievances, including taxation without consent, the multiplication of revenue officers, and the unconstitutional use of the army. Central to the whole document, however, is the reaction to the decision of the British Government to allot £1,500 annually out of the American revenue for the support of the governor and judiciary of Massachusetts. The American radicals, ever-mindful of the seventeenth-century constitutional struggles in Britain, were determined to see this as a deliberate attempt to tilt the balance of the constitution in favour of the executive. 'This will, if accomplished, compleat our slavery' **[doc. 16]**. What is more significant is that in such hands the crisis could not be confined to Boston, or even to Massachusetts, for at the same time, Adams, James Otis, Joseph Warren and eighteen others formed themselves into a Committee of Correspondence. This body, charged with the task of declaring the rights of America 'to the world', drew up the 'List of Infringements', which was sent in its essentials to other provinces.

To suggest the beginning of self-consciously national resistance may be extreme, but when the Virginia Assembly, prompted by Patrick Henry and Thomas Jefferson, followed suit, one may perhaps discern in these events both the stirrings of an independent statehood and the evidence of a common cause. The colonial governors at least, although their anxiety to get further support always led them into some exaggeration, were in little doubt, and their despatches are full of warnings that the more extreme colonial leaders were aiming at independence; but ministers at home clearly preferred to believe that the situation in Massachusetts was a special one. Early in 1773 they were already discussing the shape of stronger measures to deal with it, but by the end of the year events in Boston which had their roots on the other side of the world had overtaken them and brought the empire to its final crisis.

In May 1773, in order to help the East India Company out of its current financial difficulties, all duties levied on tea re-exported from England were remitted, and the Company was given the right to set up its own selling agencies in the colonies. There can be little doubt that the English ministers hoped also to destroy the illicit Dutch trade, and by presenting the colonists with an uncomfortable choice between their tea and their principles, force them to accept, in practice at least, the one remaining Townshend measure. It showed once more a dangerous stubbornness; an opposition proposal that the duty should be repealed as an earnest of good will and the duties remitted retained in England to provide a general imperial fund, was rejected because it cut right across what had become the fixed and central policy of the administration, that of building up in the colonies themselves a large revenue which could be used to reduce the power of their assemblies. It was an inept measure, for the allocation of the new agencies to chosen and privileged merchants, some of whom were related to members of the colonial establishment, was bound to draw justified protest from the others, some of whom now faced ruin; and while the motives behind American opposition were mixed — ranging from the anxiety of the smuggler to defend his gains, through the legitimate fear of the business man, to the desire of the patriot to take an opportunity of upholding an important constitutional principle — both merchant and radical were driven closer together in the common effort to prevent the landing of the tea.

Of this there were many instances; but in Boston, in December 1773, the day before customs officers would have seized the cargoes for non-payment of duty and possibly also because it was felt by the perpetrators that many Bostonians would in fact have bought the tea had it landed, three shiploads were dumped into the harbour by American patriots wearing Indian dress. The Boston Tea Party, against the background of the whole year, put in its most serious form yet the issue of the defiance of British power. The North administration, strengthened by the accession of many of the Grenvillites after the death of their leader in 1771, and with the firm support of a king now determined that authority should be asserted, decided on a firm policy; and since legal action against individual Americans would be difficult to apply, they brought into being a whole new machinery of parliamentary repression which would make retreat virtually impossible.

In the first months of 1774 what the Americans came to know as the 'Intolerable Acts' were passed. The Boston Port Act closed the city to commerce until the East India Company should have been compensated for the lost tea. The Administration of Justice Act gave the governors discretion to allow royal officials accused of a capital offence to stand trial outside the colony in which it had been committed, and probably in England. The Quartering Act gave them wide powers of finding billets for troops, if necessary in private houses, and extended the obligation to all the colonies. There were few in the House who seemed willing to point out the dangers involved in punishing the innocent with the guilty; or that the Quartering Act might extend the area of national resistance by visiting the sins of Boston on the colonies as a whole.

But the most serious issues of all were raised by the Massachusetts Government Act [doc. 17]. The Governor, soon to be Gage himself, was now to nominate the council which had hitherto been elected by the lower house, or General Court, and his executive power was thereby immeasurably strengthened. He was also to be responsible for recommending to the king the appointments of judges of the Supreme Court; and he was to appoint on his own initiative all local officials and lesser officers of the law who had previously been nominated by the assembly. Juries, now to be summoned by sheriffs appointed by the Governor, were to be selected with greater care. Town Meetings – to Americans the cherished grass roots of New England democracy, to the British the source of all sedition – were to meet no more than once a year and to limit their discussion to local matters.

The smouldering fear of the conspiracy to subvert American liberties now caught fire (45). Of what value was a charter, seen up to now as almost part of a solemn compact between king and people, if it could be set aside by the arbitrary decision of Parliament; what power of legislation remained in an assembly which, while it could still meet, saw Parliament, with a dangerously new grip on the internal administration of Massachusetts, now able to tax as it wished and use the revenue to pay the official puppets it appointed; and, if redress were to be sought, of what use was an appeal to a legal system so clearly controlled by the Crown? Such dependence on the Parliament of Great Britain indicated a constitutional straitjacket that the Americans were not prepared to tolerate. The long struggle which had begun over the ambiguities of taxation was about to end in the unmistakable issues of tyranny.

There was small prospect of any other policy. While Burke vainly urged a return to the compromise of 1766, he wrote privately and despairingly to the New York assembly that the popular tide was running strongly against America and that there was a general feeling that an assertion of authority was overdue. Yet, once more, the assertion was applied with little sense; the prelude to the Massachusetts Government Act held that free elections had weakened the loyalty of the moderates and made them powerless against the extremists, but it would have been difficult to devise a scheme more likely to throw them together, as Chatham pointed out in the debate on the Quartering Act in May 1774 [doc. 18]. Yet there was general support for Gage's installation as military governor with greatly increased forces. The tyranny of the Act and the military factor that would become so vital in enforcing it would do much to bind the Americans into a continental movement; and this was made more certain by the passing of another important statute which, while it was intended by Parliament almost entirely for the regulation of long-overdue matters in Canada, would be regarded by many Americans as a vital instalment of that repressive legislation by which they believed their liberties were being undermined.

5 Canada and the American Revolution

The Canadian and American provinces presented closely linked aspects of the same problem. They had a common frontier and had inevitably to meet over the question of the interior. The Board of Trade Report of 1763 had suggested that westward expansion should be reserved for the Canadians, and when the Proclamation gave effect to this and limited American expansion to the watershed of the Appalachians, it brought the first signs of that feeling among the colonists that the Canadians had been assigned a special position by the home government in the future settlement of the western lands.

There was another equally important and potentially divisive aspect of the Canadian question. As in India in 1763, Britain had acquired new territories containing people who were dissimilar to her own in race, religion and law. Her treatment of the French Canadians would be materially affected by the developing situation in the North American continent as a whole, while, conversely, the policies she adopted towards them would be closely watched by American radicals in case they gave any evidence of further favouritism, or showed any sign of attempts to win the support in the north that would enable her to exert further pressure in the south.

There already existed some 2,000 British settlers in Canada, chiefly merchants, and they were deeply concerned after 1763 to be reassured that the special position held by British law and customs would be unchanged and that they would be given fully representative government. There were now two traditions in Canada, however, and the granting of representative institutions from which the French would be excluded under the terms of the Test Act, would create a 'minority' problem of such dimensions as to make such government unworkable. The Shelburne proposals of 1768 did envisage, with some foresight, a limited share for the French in a measure of representative government; but Sir Guy Carleton, who was appointed Governor in the same year, saw with equal perception that if the British Government established a legislature in Canada she would soon be faced with the problems which were bedevilling her relations with the Americans, and essentially with the difficult task of defining the proper constitutional relationship between her own Parliament and the Canadian assembly.

Yet it was the worsening of these problems south of the border after 1770 that forced the North administration to increase its efforts to find stability in Canada. There were by then two more reasons for doing so. First, there was the growing fear in official minds that it would be difficult to keep the loyalty of the French Canadians in the event of a war between Britain and the American colonies and, worse still, France, without the grant of adequate civil liberties; second, there was the urgent need to find a revenue in Canada in view of the steady drain on British resources and of the continued failure to get anything out of the Americans. But it was again Carleton who, while he supported a programme of legal and religious toleration, advised that any Canadian assembly formed for the specific purpose of raising money would confront Britain with the same problem as those in America, with the added complication of racial antagonism. It was for this reason that another recommendation for representative government with French participation, this time in a Board of Trade report of 1769, was shelved.

After 1772 the desperate seriousness of the American question made a Canadian settlement imperative, and it was from this premise that the North administration went on to the Quebec Act of 1774; its origins were therefore defensive, however much the Americans would regard it as provocative. It settled purely Canadian questions by granting religious toleration and the use of French civil law alongside English criminal law; administration was to be through a legislative council to be nominated by the Crown which was to work with the governor; and the Test Act was suspended in the province to make it possible for the French Canadians to be given nine of its twenty places, with eight allocated to the British settlers, and three filled by officials who, nominated by the governor, usually turned out to be sympathetic to the French. Yet the bitter experiences of the attempt to govern the American colonies was clearly in the minds of the men who framed the measure, for while the legislative body was to be allowed to share in law-making, it was not to authorise taxation; revenue was to come from the regulation of trade.

The Act brought American and Canadian issues most closely together by extending the jurisdiction of the Governor of Quebec into the interior. It was a plain and straightforward recognition of the fact that with the administration of the American colonies so near to collapse, North America as a whole would have to be governed from Canada. The area to be thus supervised was to extend north and west of a line from the valley of the St Lawrence, through Lakes Ontario and Erie, and thence down the Ohio and along to the Mississippi, skirting the western boundaries of Pennsylvania and Virginia. The prime consideration was the need to bring orderly government to isolated settlements of some 1,500 French Canadians in the west whose existence was barely realised in 1763, and to win their loyalty by giving them the civil rights that were to be accorded to Quebec; not far behind was the perennial wish to protect the fur trade and reduce the chances of a frontier war by easing the pressure on the Indian tribes. That pressure, however, was coming in the main from the older American colonies; and while in imperial terms the Quebec Act could be seen as an attempt to solve the problems of the interior which had so far been obstructed by the American resistance to taxation, and by a reluctance to accept the logic of the Shelburne proposals, it could only be regarded by the colonists as an act of intentional provocation.

For the challenge of the frontier had not been taken up. The excellent Indian Service had been greatly reduced, and the simultaneous establishment of a more generous limit on westward expansion suggests that the British ministers believed that in the absence of sufficient funds to do anything else, this was the best way of restraining movement into the interior. In fact, they had done no more than open the way for more bitter conflicts between the backwoodsmen and the Indians. A reasonably organised attempt to penetrate the whole Ohio area from West Virginia, the shortlived Vandalia project patronised by Franklin, was abandoned. Such colonisation was of the kind envisaged in the Shelburne proposals, but it was clearly inconsistent with the policy laid down in the Board of Trade Report of 1768, and it was stifled by the growing dislike of Franklin in ministerial circles; more important was the hostility of the Virginians towards it, for they, the most restless of the colonists, had earmarked these territories for themselves.

Between 1768 and 1772 they pushed hard against the Cherokee, and fear of a general Indian war led Stuart, almost the last representative of the old Indian Service, to persuade the Indians to give up all their claims as far as the Kentucky River. Then, in the piecemeal expansion that was clearly going on apace, the Shawnee surrendered all their claims south of the Ohio; in the process George Washington, a colonel in the Virginia militia in the Seven Years War and acquiring then thousands of acres of land, now added considerably more to them. By 1774 Richard Henderson, in defiance of regulations of all kinds, had through the Transylvanian Company settled much of Kentucky and pushed the western boundary as far as the Mississippi.

There had thus been an almost entirely illicit movement to the west, by evasion or *ad hoc* adjustments. Thus, while the origins of the American Revolution are not to be found entirely in the issues of taxation and constitutional rights that arose mainly in the tidewater, it would be quite inaccurate to suggest that in the offence it gave to frontiersmen and land speculators, the halting and ineffective frontier policy of the British was anything like as important. The broad question of the new lands had of course raised in its immediate form the whole question of taxation; but for the rest it had so far been no more than a source of annoyance and irritation.

The frontier provisions of the Quebec Act, however, come into a different category, and when they are considered together with its specifically Canadian clauses and placed against the background of the coercive legislation of 1774, they form a vital element in a much more dangerous pattern of resentment. For once more the Americans sniffed the 'tainted breeze of tyranny', this time blowing from the north. An unrepresentative government in Canada was to be sustained by French civil law and by a religion which was especially repulsive to the New Englanders; it was to be buttressed by the creation of Popish settlements to the north and west of the Americans which would block the natural and legitimate expansion of a people who were already beginning to feel the promptings of their manifest destiny. To the Americans, in the light of the coercion they were experiencing and of the instructions to the Royal Governors of February 1774, to put tighter control on further expansion to the west, the Quebec Act seemed no more than an attempt to check Protestant freedom and expansion by the promotion of a clerical autocracy in the north, and, whether filled by Indians or Papists (between whom the Americans seemed little inclined to distinguish) a hostile power in the west.

The primary purpose of the Act was in fact none of these things, but its timing gave it all the appearance of being so. As it was being debated in the Commons, news of the Boston Tea Party reached London and brought stronger demands for retaliation; and while Camden, Chatham and Charles James Fox pointed out the provocation contained in the Act, others were quite happy to see it as a means of stifling a growing spirit of independence. Across the Atlantic, the news of its passing reached the colonies as the First Continental Congress was about to meet, and Gage warned correctly that it made the people 'generally ripe for any plan the Congress might advise'. The extremist cause was strengthened, and a substantial platform was given to those radicals who were already seeking to link the grievances of Massachusetts to the aspirations of a new nation; and it made the task of Gage, already planning in military terms to achieve the isolation of the radical coastal areas, markedly more difficult. For, of all the measures of 1774, the Quebec Act could be the most easily represented as a threat to the security of every one of the thirteen colonies.

PART THREE

The Crisis, 1774-76

6 First Continental Congress 1774

Attitudes on both sides thus hardened in the fires of the disputes of 1774. A sharp antithesis had emerged, and while there were still moderates in America, as there were still Whig and radical friends of the colonists in Britain, any real hope of reconciliation depended on whether these advocates of good sense would be allowed to find common ground. Such firm and unyielding positions had been taken up on either side, however, that the area of compromise had grown desperately small.

In Britain political stability had been found at last, and with it a consistent American policy which had for that reason to be severe **(55)**. The debate was no longer about the niceties of taxation and representation; there was now near unanimity that British sovereignty had to be applied and the meaning of the Declaratory Act made clear. George III's conviction that the Americans needed discipline was reinforced by the result of the election of 1774, when the solid support of the ministry – Grenvillites, country gentlemen, ex-officers and colonial servants – would have agreed with their ruler 'that the fatal compliance in 1766 has encouraged the Americans annually to encrease in their pretensions that thorough independency which one State has of another, but which is quite subversive of the obedience which a Colony owes to its Mother Country' **(3)**. Now, moreover, there seemed little inclination towards compromise among the merchant classes, and in so far as some of them counted the value of their growing trade with Europe and the rest of the world, and doubted the worth of colonies that could be retained only at great expense, this attitude suggests that the economic mortar of the first British empire was already crumbling and that there was already a significant move towards free trade **[doc. 28]** .

The urgent advice of the men on the spot was now heeded. Gage reached Boston in May with instructions to enforce the coercive laws. The first Massachusetts General Court he convened revealed that both assembly and council were determined to recover chartered rights and, in the short time before it was dissolved, anxious to take the lead in the summoning of a continental congress; while the nominated councillors by whom they were replaced in September were for the most part induced to resign under threat of violence. Unlawful town meetings were then held, and the radicals, led by Sam Adams, began to prepare the ground for further non-importation agreements. The threat of force was never far from their proceedings, and resolutions passed in Suffolk County, which contained Boston, openly urged military preparations in defence of colonial rights. By then Gage was calling for more troops, pointing to the growing illicit trade with the Indians, the wholesale penetration of the frontier and the organised resistance to quartering. His influence at this time was vital. He had consistently deplored a lack of policy. In 1769 he wrote to Barrington, Secretary-at-War:

> From the denying the right of internal taxations, they next deny the right of duties on imports, and thus they mean to go on step by step, 'till they throw off all subjection to your laws. They will acknowledge the King of Great Britain to be their King, but soon deny the prerogative of the Crown, and acknowledge their King no longer than it shall be convenient for them to do so.'

In 1770 his had been the decisive voice against a further movement of the frontier; he deplored the possibility of new inland colonies, insisting that it was the function of his men 'to protect the settlements and keep the settlers in subjection to the government'. By 1774 he was convinced that there was a plot to seize independence, and believed that its roots were in Massachusetts. Other colonial governors and their officials concurred, and there was a general belief among them that British administration was on the point of collapse (41).

In America, widespread support for Massachusetts was growing, for no colony could but feel that its traditional liberties were in danger. There was still loyalty and moderation, but when Franklin at this point expressed the belief that all would yet be well if Britain dropped its claims to tax he was showing in his very moderation that there was a growing body of American opinion in favour at least of a radical restatement of the colonial relationship. Beneath, and equally significantly, there was a substantial minority anxious to see its complete abandonment.

The line between the two was not sharp, but as extremism in Britain had become impatient of evasion, so had that in America become more highly organised. Through the growing Committees of Correspondence and the Sons of Liberty, those who believed in freedom — whether in legal and constitutional terms or in the opportunity it would give to smuggle, to expand, not to pay taxes, or even simply to riot — found themselves falling more and more under the sway of an active minority which was fostering a growing contempt for British authority. More significantly, it was laying claim to a new body of doctrine whose evolution may be marked through the pages of one writer after another — through Otis, Dulany and Dickinson — and which was about to reach its logical end. Gage, in his direct way, was right, for the denial of the power to tax internally must bring into question the foundation of British sovereignty in general. If there was no constitutional authority for the raising of a revenue, then from what source did Parliament derive its right to legislate at all?

Throughout 1774 a distinctively Whig view was being built up. Relations between Britain and the colonies before 1756, it seemed to suggest, had been based on mutual, even contractual, consent; but now the British seemed determined to destroy the balance of that relationship fundamentally and unilaterally, first by extracting an unconstitutional revenue, directly or indirectly, and second by sustaining a corps of hostile officials and a menacing army with the proceeds. A threat so great could be met only jointly. It would be done first by a plea for a more generous statement of the imperial relationship; but if this negative, though fundamental demand for what were still regarded as the rights of Englishmen could not be satisfied within the empire, it was highly unlikely that it would cease.

CHATHAM AND BURKE — I

The chances of creating a new imperial framework seemed remote, for there was little in the reaction to the famous speeches made by Chatham and Burke in the spring of 1774 to suggest the possibility of new thinking in Britain. Yet neither could be entirely positive. Chatham's views, for example, are not easy to summarise, for they are those of a Whig who was also an imperialist; indeed, he had done more than any other living man to create the empire whose future was now being debated so urgently. This dichotomy comes out clearly in the debates over the Declaratory Act of 1766, for while he insisted that Britain had no right to tax the colonies, advancing Whig principles 'of that old order which placed the fundamental law of the constitution beyond the reach of Parliament', he believed at the same time that her sovereign authority over the empire should be expressed in the strongest possible terms (20). Later in the debate, in reply to Grenville, he maintained that America's struggle for freedom was also Britain's, and the question of taxation was an essential part of both; he did not accept the official case for virtual representation, for to the true Whig Parliament was too corrupt even to represent its own people adequately. Yet, once more, comes the demand for an assertion of sovereignty: 'the greater must govern the less' by using 'power sovereign and supreme': but there is no apparent thought of how weak that sovereign power would become if taxation were to be subtracted from it.

Yet in the same speech there is the most clear analysis of the question of taxation which showed full sympathy with the American view and which, properly interpreted, might have led to more imaginative British policies. All levies, whether internal or external, were rejected if their essential purpose was the collection of a revenue; but the imperial vision remains in the insistence that the power to regulate trade would be of enormous mutual benefit, and that a wisely applied supervisory control would halt the drift to civil war which would destroy the empire and restore the fortunes of the Bourbons. One is inevitably led to consider the paradox of the doomed ministry of 1766 over which Chatham lost control. There was no generous imperial reconstruction and no concession of the power to tax; instead, merely the rejection of the opportunity offered by the Shelburne plan to take the Americans into continental partnership, and the failure to restrain Townshend from insisting that all taxation was within the province of the British Parliament and from going on to destroy the empire.

In opposition again, in January 1770, shortly before the formation of North's ministry, the voice of the true Whig was heard once more. Like Englishmen, Chatham maintained, the Americans were right to protest against bad law, for this was the only way it could be changed. And in 1774, when moderation was so badly needed, he once more denied the right to tax. While he was also Whig enough to condemn mob violence, he believed that such protests proceeded from the fundamental error of the tea tax, and that there were enough moderate Americans to ensure a better imperial relationship provided they were not lumped together with the wrongdoers in blanket condemnation and punishment [doc. 18a]. Yet the denial of the right to tax still constituted a vital subtraction from authority, and if the sovereignty of Parliament over colonial assemblies could not be asserted or accepted, then there remained only the possibility that some imperial connection could endure under the Crown; and while this was a view which would find fuller expression in the writings of contemporary Americans, the idea that the monarchy which they believed to be so closely involved in Indian and domestic patronage should play a significant role in imperial politics could find little place in the Whig philosophy of Chatham and Burke.

Burke, unlike Chatham, was not disposed to distinguish between what Parliament could and could not do; and while in 1769, in his *Observation on a Late Publication intituled The Present State of the*

Nation, he sets out the problem of the mercantile empire whose parts ultimately had to be given meaning and order, he would not concede that the Stamp Act had been repealed because it was constitutionally invalid: if the right to tax was to be legally surrendered, then 'the presiding authority of Great Britain, as the head, the arbiter, and director of the whole empire, would vanish into an empty name, without operation or energy' (3). But this right, even if constitutionally valid, should be used with all restraint, for without this the Americans could not remain free. The Stamp Act had been repealed on the grounds of equity and expediency, and because reasonable men had seen such a course to be correct. Burke would return constantly to the fine balance which he believed had been struck in 1766; but it would not be easy to maintain in a changing situation, and it would be destroyed for ever by the policies of Charles Townshend.

Yet after all the difficulties those policies brought, in the spring months of 1774 Burke was still trying to save British policy from its obsession with legality, for while he believed that sensible and fair practice had made the prewar colonial system tolerable, the inflexible theories of Grenville and Townshend had made it unbearable. He was therefore in practice ready to accept the American distinction between internal and external levies, maintaining that the latter should be confined to the regulation of trade alone and the Americans allowed to tax themselves for internal purposes. Burke thus moved in practice towards the theoretical position of Chatham, and then further, towards his first examination of the difficult question of sovereignty. He perceived that the American colonies had a separate and developing life, and that their people were claiming rights which would have to be scrupulously examined if they were not to provide a rapidly worsening problem for succeeding generations; leniency and magnanimity would not be enough, and he saw, without offering a comprehensive solution, that the matter of reconciling the imperial rights of the British with the rights of the Americans would be the vital question of the future.

If sovereignty could not be divided precisely, then the Imperial Parliament should be given two functions. The first was as the legislature for Britain itself; the second, its imperial role, was to guide the colonial legislatures towards the common enjoyment of the liberty shared by Englishmen all over the world. It was by no means a precise idea, and it did not involve a categorical diminution of sovereignty – there had to be reserve power in the empire which could, in times of extremity, make up for the deficiencies which might appear in its parts; but there is for the first time on the British side the suggestion of the imperial framework of the future [doc. 18] . Like so much of the British constitution as it existed then, and the Commonwealth as it would develop, it would involve much that was assumed and unwritten, intuitively arrived at, and only capable of being put into practice by the exercise of the utmost good sense and understanding. These qualities were rare at the end of the eighteenth century.

WILSON AND JEFFERSON

These were not to be the last pleas made by Burke and Chatham for common sense. They would fail, as Gladstone would in Ireland a century later, because the more successfully they clarified the ambiguities which surrounded the problem, the more clearly did they expose the fundamental issues at its heart. So also from the American side were men of good faith and constructive views being led towards the view that the vital matter of sovereignty was virtually insoluble within the existing framework of empire.

The writings of James Wilson and Thomas Jefferson present a historical problem in themselves, for it is difficult to be sure how much general support there was among Americans for the persuasive views of these highly articulate men, and whether, with more understanding on the British side, a sufficient number of Americans would have been found to make them workable. But in the light of the vacuum created by the lack of a constructive British policy, their views become highly significant, and it is reasonable to suggest that both writers represent, on the eve of the calling of the First Continental Congress of 1774, a general rejection of the claims of parliamentary sovereignty.

In his *Considerations on the Authority of Parliament* of August 1774, Wilson wrote that he had begun his work in the hope of being able to distinguish between the areas in which the Americans should and should not acknowledge the authority of Parliament. His conclusion was set out with devastating simplicity: careful thought had convinced him that such a line could not be drawn and that there was 'no medium between acknowledging and denying that power in all cases'. The bleak antithesis, already posed so clearly by extremists – by Dr Johnson, in whose sovereignty there were no gradations, and by Grenville and Townshend on the one hand, and by John Adams on the other – which had lurked half-hidden beneath the writings of moderate men on both sides, was now plain for all to see, and it was the extreme solution that was likely to prevail.

Wilson went on to a vital deduction. If there was no legal obligation to accept the authority of Parliament, then even the right to regulate trade came not from the sovereign position of the mother country but from implied commercial compacts between her and the colonies [**doc. [19]**]. It stressed once more the contractual nature of the colonial relationship, and it would be heard again in the Declaration of Rights of the First Continental Congress in October when it admitted 'cheerful consent' to the Laws of Trade, and therefore suggested that the authority of Parliament to apply them was in a sense conferred on it by the colonies themselves [**doc. 21**]. It marked again the crumbling of the mercantilist position, and provided the basis for the free commercial association of an independent America with Britain which Shelburne was at pains to promote in 1782, and which could never have been achieved without abandoning sovereignty.

If parliamentary sovereignty was thus to be rejected, then the Americans were no more than fellow-subjects with the British, and their only possible loyalty was therefore owed to the king; and Wilson would have reserved to him the duty of supervising foreign relations and commerce, and restraining all the assemblies of the empire so as to guarantee to all his subjects the same degree of liberty and individual rights. It is superficially close to the views expressed by Burke in the same year, with the highly important difference that Burke would have given these functions to the Imperial Parliament. In the form put forward by Wilson, its chances of a sympathetic hearing in England were remote, for it was quite impossible for English moderates to assign these duties to a ruler whom they believed to be so heavily involved in the day-to-day management of English politics; the success of what may be termed the Commonwealth idea would rest first on a common loyalty towards a totally impartial ruler, and second on the growth of a form of responsible government in Britain in which the sovereign would become little more than a figurehead. The frustrating paradox of the moderate attitude towards the American crisis was that the better Whig a man was, the less able was he to accept the concept of linked and equal sovereignties presided over by a ruler he knew only in eighteenth-century terms. At the same time an equally formidable barrier to Wilson's ideas was about to be created on the American side, for the illusion that the only tyranny suffered by the colonists was a parliamentary one was about to be stripped away.

Thomas Jefferson's *A Summary View of the Rights of British America* was drafted in August 1774 as the basis of instructions for the Virginian delegates to the First Continental Congress, and in pamphlet form it had very considerable influence. It ranged ably and persuasively over the past grievances of the Americans; it claimed legislative competence for the colonies themselves, and once more appealed to the king as 'Chief Magistrate' to use his prerogative to curb the parliamentary power that bore so heavily on his colonial subjects. There is, however, a significant development in thought, for the rights to be thus protected were held to derive from the laws of nature [doc. 20]. This would be too much for many of the delegates to the First Congress to accept, but it would achieve general approval in the Declaration of Independence, and it began to move the colonial argument away from the family quarrel about the rights of Englishmen, about which the North administration had quite different ideas of its own, and in which deadlock had been reached, into the field of the natural rights which it would be theoretically easier to assert, and towards the political ideas which produced the Enlightenment and the French Revolution.

FIRST CONGRESS

Delegates from all the colonies except Georgia gathered in Philadelphia in September 1774 to form a Congress which, as it assembled, bore few of the marks of a self-conscious political body. But in the excitement of these autumn months, and against the background of economic frustration, one would grow, supported by a mood of fraternity and political fervour which would lead the delegates to face squarely the issues of independence. Its economic programme alone, for example, forced a good measure of intercolonial agreement; the non-importation of British goods was to begin on 1 December 1774; a total ban on exports to Britain on 10 September 1775; and the Continental Association which was established to implement the embargo became also the parent of the many Committees of Safety all over the colonies which had the task of enforcing it. They were to be the marker flags of the new nation.

Political agreement would not be so easy, for Congress faced the formidable task of defining in practice the nature of the rights on which it stood. Were they to call upon their Charters, or upon their English heritage, or were they to cut through the tangle of constitutional debate and claim the sanction of a universal natural law that must inevitably lead them into renouncing that heritage? This was a relatively easier task for theorists like Wilson than for an assembly of delegates from so many different areas; and even if they could agree on this, how would they prevail upon an English administration to treat with them? If, finally, a mutual recognition of a new position could not be secured within the empire, with what unanimity would they approach the awesome task of cutting their links with it? Such matters would not be easy to decide in a gathering which is estimated to have contained broadly equal representation of those of conservative, radical and neutral views. While there is evidence to suggest that there were delegates of substance who wanted to avert a social revolution by inspiring patriotic feelings, the conservative group consisted largely of those who wanted no more than a more favourable statement of the imperial relationship and of the rights of Englishmen. The radicals wanted a greater degree of separation, and while many of them would have followed Wilson and Jefferson in denying the competence of the English Parliament in their internal affairs, and looked to the establishment of separate imperial communities joined under some barely specified royal supervision, the difficulty of defining it, and the imminent realisation that the king was firmly behind the policies of his ministers, would make this but a brief stopping place on the path towards complete separation.

Power in such raw gatherings, full of grievance and conscious of facing a rare moment of destiny, will invariably swing towards the left, as it did in France in 1789. The conservative ranks were hesitant. Dickinson stood staunchly by his earlier views, but urged caution in action. Joseph Galloway produced a plan for union between Britain and the colonies as an alternative to the radical programme, containing, in a reversion to the mood of the Albany Plan, the suggestion for the setting up of a Grand Council to be elected by members of the colonial assemblies, with full competence in American affairs, and subject only to the veto of a Resident-General appointed by the king; but it was rejected by one vote, partly because it would have involved a degree of subordination to Britain unacceptable to many of the delegates, partly because it would have meant the sacrifice of more intercolonial independence than the separate American communities could yet envisage (1). While it suggested in outline something of the position that the colonies would eventually have to assume, its rejection was the first evidence that Congress was ready to take up a more extreme position.

The second was in its Declaration and Resolves of October. There was still no clear agreement about the derivation of the rights the delegates claimed, and they were ascribed without much discrimination to their charters, to their English lineage and to natural rights [doc. 21]. It was, however, strongly worded, and it established a position from which retreat would be difficult. It came out fully behind Massachusetts in its decision to defy the legislation of 1774; the American assemblies asked for no less than full legislative competence within their own borders; there should be no standing army without their consent; they were entitled to all the benefits of the common law; and all the legislation which had so deeply offended them since 1763 should be totally repealed. There is here a clear and fundamental wish to go back to the years before the Seven Years War, to the golden age in which it was believed that these rights had existed in fact; and in their attitude of 'cheerful consent' to trade regulation and in the absence of any discussion of Indian or defence policy there is evidence still that the Americans who gave their support to the Declaration, determined as they were to recover their rights, were not yet fully prepared to act as an independent community.

The third sign of the movement towards a more radical position came with the general adoption of the Suffolk County Resolves, written by Joseph Warren, who was to lose his life at Bunker Hill, and forced on Congress by Sam Adams [doc. 22]. They insisted not only on there being a repeal of recent Acts of Parliament, but on there being no general obligation to obey them. Their assumption by Congress was an implied approval of the resistance already offered in Boston and a clear hint that such force, in similar conditions, could be generally and legitimately applied.

7 Second Continental Congress 1775

Both sides had thus reached positions in the early months of 1775 which brought war very clearly into sight. In the colonies independence was now a burning issue in both press and pulpit; drilling was common, a militia was being organised, and Washington gained his first substantial military appointment as Commander-in-Chief of the Virginian armies. In January, in the *Novanglus Papers,* John Adams restated what had by then become the common currency of the radical argument: that the colonies, while they owed allegiance to the king, were entirely beyond the competence of Parliament, and that the least abhorrent relationship to Britain was the one which he claimed had worked to the benefit of the colonies for some 150 years, giving the British Parliament the right to regulate trade alone, 'and our assemblies all other matters' [doc. 23]. Yet a return to the salutary neglect of the Walpole era, to that golden age which had a particular appeal to the more moderate colonists, was out of the question; it had been preserved only by stealth on the one side and acquiescence on the other, and both had since quite openly taken up positions from which there could be no retreat. Indeed the strictures addressed by Franklin to Galloway in a letter of February 1775 give some indication of the distaste which was developing in the colonies for any closer links with a political system as corrupt as that of Britain was held generally to have become, and even of the moral superiority that would persuade many Americans that they were destined to create a more vital form of the freedom that had once inspired Englishmen [doc. 24].

What the American leadership was claiming, whether in the form of a new relationship which they could not properly define, or in a reversion to an old one which had never been carefully examined, was full legislative independence; yet what English ruling opinion now believed to be necessary was a clear statement of the legislative authority without which the empire would collapse. The administration acted, too late, with determination but also with provocation. In January colonial governors were instructed to prevent the election of delegates to a second Continental Congress, and the New England colonies were deemed to be in a state of rebellion. In March the New England Restraining Act limited the commerce of these colonies rigidly to Britain and the West Indies. Throughout these months, British military power was being built up, in spite of Chatham's warning that it would be largely ineffective. Concessions from the British Government were now likely to be limited, and they would in any case quite clearly depend upon the acceptance by the colonists of what North termed 'the constitutional right of supremacy'.

CHATHAM AND BURKE – II

The task of those who still sought reconciliation was harder. Chatham was impelled to try once more; in January 1775 he moved in the Lords for the withdrawal of the army from Boston on the grounds that it could hope for no more than a partial and shortlived conquest, and might well inflict the first bloodshed that would be a 'wound beyond cure', while its evacuation would be a token of a wish to conciliate, even to repeal the oppressive laws of 1774. But the British mood did not incline to the modification of either her military presence or her legal claims, and in vain did Chatham appeal once more to a fundamental Whiggism as he reminded his listeners that American resistance should have been foreseen by the descendants of those Englishmen who had challenged the Stuarts and established the absolute basis of a free society, that no man should be taxed save by his own consent. In effect, he accepted the prevailing American view, praising a Congress which contained men too mature to accept any other sort of relationship.

In February he introduced a more detailed measure for settling the troubles in America. The repressive legislation of 1774 should be suspended and the right of taxation renounced; freedom before the law was to be restored by a reaffirmation of trial by jury and a limitation on the powers of the Vice-Admiralty Courts, and by a promise to appoint judges on the same terms as in England – during their good behaviour rather than at the king's pleasure; while an assurance should be given that the army would not be used in any way that would endanger the rights of the people. But this went nowhere near the claim of Congress that troops should not be sent to any of the colonies without the consent of its assembly, and when Chatham suggested that the colonies should recognise the legislative authority of Parliament in all matters except taxation, and as an earnest of their own good faith should consider assigning to the king a perpetual revenue over and above that required for the administration of each colony, which could be disposed of by Parliament so as to ease the financial difficulties of the mother country, there could be little response. For while the national character of Congress would be recognised to the extent that it would determine the proportion of the charge to be borne by each colony, it is far from certain that this qualified acceptance would have overcome the distaste of many of its members for a recognition of British sovereignty and a free grant to the King-in-Parliament, in spite of the approximation of a good number of the Chatham proposals to the Congress resolutions of the previous October. What is quite certain is that had it not been defeated in the House of Lords by sixty-one votes to thirty-two, it would have been overwhelmingly rejected by a House of Commons which, since the election of 1774, was almost united in its demand for the assertion of total British supremacy.

In March Burke made his great speech on conciliation, urging that serious thought should be given to concessions offered in peace and magnanimity **(6)**. For he believed that it was impossible to change the temper of the Americans, so deeply rooted in their reverence for political and religious freedom, and that punitive methods had failed because there was 'no method of drawing up an indictment against a whole people'. Yet while the essence of conciliation remained the attempt to define the power and functions of the colonial assemblies, he admitted that the distinction between these and the authority of the British Parliament would be a most difficult one to draw. In economic terms it was easy. Levies from trade regulation could be taken to represent the colonial contribution towards imperial expenses, while for the support of their own establishments they should be allowed to tax themselves. It was in the definition of political and civil liberties that the difficulties would lie, and Burke could do no more than suggest that they should be identified with those of Englishmen and guaranteed by a constitution of universal validity, with no suggestion that the power of the mother country should be evaluated in terms different to those which set out the privileges of the colonies. The sovereign authority of Parliament should have imperial meaning in the sense that it should be applied chiefly to the vital task of preserving common and long-standing liberties on both sides of the Atlantic.

Yet if the supreme power was not to be abandoned, however wisely it was to be used, it would have to take the initiative in setting out the pattern of any new relationship. It was hardly likely that the patriot leaders, in the mood of these early months of 1775, would be prepared to allow any outside body to define the extent of their liberties for them, and it may here be appropriate to suggest that Burke, while Colonial Agent for New York, was linked with the most conservative of all the colonies and was never fully aware of the intensity of radical feeling elsewhere. It was at the same time a highly imaginative proposal,

71

and the fabric it sought to weave so delicate that only statesmanship of a very high order could possibly have sustained it. Burke conceded that the 'vulgar, mechanical politicians', conditioned by the old assumptions of political and economic power, could not possibly have embraced it, but he hoped that some would instinctively understand. Yet few were ready to make the effort, and the resolutions he sponsored in the House were defeated by 270 votes to 78 (3).

The failure of Burke and Chatham illustrates once more the enormous gulf which had opened between Britain and her colonies. They would be heard again after the war had begun, but with voices even fainter. In his letter to the Bristol Sheriffs in 1777, Burke had yielded not one particle in his 'zeal for the supremacy of Parliament'. In theory it could not be qualified, but it should in practice be applied with reserve. It had to exist, if for no other reason than that the Americans occupied only a part of a highly complex empire – it was for Burke, for example, the only instrument strong enough to impose reform on India, with which he was equally preoccupied – but it should be used 'to reconcile the strong, presiding power that is so useful towards the conservation of a vast, disconnected, infinitely diversified empire, with the liberty and safety of the provinces, which they must enjoy'. Again, it was an imaginative concept, but well beyond the reach of orthodox eighteenth-century thought (5). Chatham also, in 1777, still sought to apply his fundamental Whiggism to the colonies; they were rebels, but in the right cause, and should be conciliated for the sake of the happiness of British subjects all over the world (3). In the end, however, in the last frail intervention of 1778, the imperialist in him was revived; the entry of France and Spain into the war made it imperative that there should be no surrender of the imperial possessions.

Comparison is inevitable, for they had much in common. Their insight into the problem was a profound one, and both scorned the legal expedients and hand-to-mouth solutions of the men actually responsible for the handling of American affairs over these years; neither would concede that the idea of virtual representation could offer any solution to the problem, and both were critical enough of the English political system to deny that it had any validity on the other side of the Atlantic.

Yet there is a difference in their approach. While both understood the depth of feeling on the American side, Chatham advanced a Whig spirit that truly belonged to the seventeenth century and put colonial claims in the setting of the development of free government in England; only he, and not Burke, could have said, 'Three millions of people so dead to all the feelings of liberty as voluntarily to submit to be slaves, would have been fit instruments to make slaves of all the rest'. Burke offered a more dispassionate examination of the very real problem of dealing with a people situated three thousand miles away, and full of the spirit of civil and religious liberty. It was a fact to be accepted, a situation to exercise the mind, rather than provide a platform for Whig policies; if it was impossible to coerce a whole nation, then the only way forward had to be through careful conciliation.

This leads to the central point, and to the fundamental difference between the two. Because, as Beloff says, Chatham was the better Whig, his emotional attachment to the American cause would hardly allow him to make the compromises through which Burke sought after conciliation. In denying absolutely the English right to tax America he left little more to be said, and when he attempted to assert sovereignty without the power of taxation, he came to an impossible position; perhaps because he was more concerned with the very real matter of the future of the empire than with the abstract right of Parliament. Burke, on the other hand, was 'zealous for the supremacy of Parliament in all respects', and the right of taxation was an essential part of it, for sovereignty was indivisible; yet in practice it should be given up, and the exercise of power dictated by reasonableness and not by law. Thus, for Burke, the Declaratory Act of 1766 was a happy compromise between theory and practice and, taken together with the Stamp Act, the acme of sound policy. Chatham would never accept that its terms extended to taxation, and came to detest it. It was, sadly for the policy of American conciliation, more than a disagreement in principle; Burke and the Rockingham Whigs never yielded in their belief in a British sovereignty which included the power to tax, and it was one of the issues which made practical cooperation between them and Chatham impossible (**20**).

Yet, this central issue apart, both thought in imperially imaginative fashion, although with different emphasis. Chatham, as the crisis approached and the war developed, seems more concerned with the practical issues of holding an empire together, critical of the day-to-day handling of affairs – of the blanket punishment of 1774, and of the use of the army. He emerges as the statesman of past power and present action, who had helped to create the empire and drive out the Bourbons, and his recommendations are essentially the immediate ones that would enable it to live: the concession of the right of taxation, the restoration of civil rights, the recognition of the Continental Congress. Burke comes out more strongly in the last stages of the crisis as the political seeker after the imperial future, suggesting the means by which it would endure. The Imperial Parliament would have two functions: to govern at home, and to safeguard the liberties of British subjects all over the world, and in this a 'nice' line should be drawn in practice between its rights, and the privileges and immunities of the lesser assemblies, which could be permitted to tax themselves internally without the concession of an absolute right to do so. Constitutional forms had to be accepted, but the interests of the empire at large could only be secured by following policies of justice and humanity and, above all, equity. In his glimpse of an aggregate of states guided by the same principles and safeguarded by a common presiding power, he reached towards the concept of dominion status and Commonwealth, built on 'ties which though light as air, are as strong as links of iron'. For while, like Chatham, he would have repealed all the legislation since 1763 which was obnoxious to the colonists, he also accepted the possibility of future growth towards the end of voluntary partnership.

Both failed bravely. Chatham's suggestions for practical and immediate concessions in 1775 were too much for most of his contemporaries, for few believed that there would be anything to bind the Americans when the right to tax had been swiftly and legally conceded, and few would understand the spirit in which Burke's arguments were put. The greatest obstacle of all to conciliation in 1775, however, was that the Americans had virtually reached the position in which they would not allow Englishmen of any sort, however well-meaning, to state for them the conditions on which the imperial relationship should be continued.

THE LAST MONTHS

Neither, of course, was anywhere near the seat of power. Lord North occupied that, and the colonists were certainly in no mood to have the extent of their liberties defined for them by the author of the repressive legislation of 1774. His 'conciliatory propositions' of February 1775 represented the limit of ministerial concession, and suggested that if the colonists would adequately and permanently support the royal officials, and would be prepared to grant a sum to Britain in time of war which was proportionate to that raised for internal purposes, then, if these conditions were always met, there would be no resort to parliamentary taxation. On the surface, it seemed to concede the principle of taxation by consent, and a minority of colonial leaders might have accepted it. The majority, however, discerned two disagreeable features; if they were to find a permanent revenue, it would rob them of the day-to-day control of their own affairs which had been slowly built up before 1763 and which they now regarded as the touchstone of their liberties; while as Benjamin Franklin among many others saw, it also amounted to taxation by threat, the language of the highwayman [**doc. 24**]. Only the fullest exercise of the ministry's power of patronage persuaded a reluctant House to consent to offer it, and there was very little that would induce the Americans to accept it.

By the spring of 1775 events were moving very quickly indeed. Repressive policies in the colonies developed to the point of requiring the suspension of any assemblies which came out in support of the colonial cause, or, in defiance of governors' instructions, made arrangements to be represented at the Second Congress. These suspensions, when they came, brought an air of finality, partly because they represented the end of compromise, partly because in so doing the royal officials were dispensing with constitutional bodies which could pass on protests in a legal way; there could be no vacuum, and the space thus created was filled by illegal assemblies which would inevitably pass from protest to an assumption of government and the recruitment of irregular military forces. As the process went on, the only expression left of British power was Gage and the army. In mid-April he received his first clear instructions to put down the rebellion; unable to take the leaders of the unconstitutional provincial assemblies, he decided instead to seize a vital dump of rebel arms at Concord, fifteen miles from Boston. As they made their way there, his troops were harried by a party of American irregulars at Lexington, and although they successfully completed their mission at Concord, they suffered considerable losses on the way home. By May there were besieged in Boston, with little hope of breaking out again.

It was in this atmosphere that the Second Continental Congress met, convinced that the British were about to impose a military solution. There was still a reluctance (reflecting the view of the country at large rather than that generally held by the delegates) to ask for full independence, representing conservative misgivings about the fast-rising power of radicalism and the possibility of mob rule, about what Governor Morris of New York described as the driving of 'the god of ambition and the goddess of faction', and John Dickinson feared that too sudden a break might divide the colonies north and south of the Hudson River. In spite of this, there was a powerful momentum. The facts of independence were becoming clear. The need to help the people of Massachusetts to defend their liberties against Gage led to the creation of the Continental Army in June, to the absorption into it of the irregular forces already besieging Boston, and to the appointment of Washington as Commander-in-Chief. At the same time those who were clear in their purpose, men like John Hancock, Benjamin Franklin, James Wilson and Thomas Jefferson, were providing the driving force which would turn the Congress from a gathering of protesting delegates into a working government with both legislative and executive branches. The new armies had to be supported, and on June 22 Congress voted to issue paper money on its own authority, and a Treasury of sorts appeared, accompanied by an Indian Commission and postal services. The imperial organisation which Britain had tried in vain to impose on the colonies was now taking shape without her.

In this setting, North's proposals were rejected out of hand as 'unreasonable and invidious', and in July the radical Jefferson and the moderate Dickinson together drafted the *Declaration of the Causes and Necessity of Taking up Arms.* It went forcefully over all the old ground, and stressed in particular the reasonable and restrained petitions which had been ignored over the past ten years, and which had left the colonists no choice but that of armed resistance. It was more extreme than any previous declaration, containing for the first time the hint that the Americans suspected the intentions of the king and the firm expression of their belief that they would not lack foreign help; yet it was still clear that they would have returned to what they believed their old relationship to have been. Two days later the moderate position in Congress crumbled away. On the insistence of Dickinson and the conservatives, some clearly still concerned about the future of an independent America under radical leadership, the famous 'olive branch' petition was sent to the king, asking for the setting up of machinery for redress, the suspension of fighting, and the repeal of the disputed legislation of the past. The radicals knew that it would gain no response, and they were correct; its rejection showed that the British Government was in no mood to build bridges towards moderate opinion and that there was no possibility of reconciliation.

Independence was clearly in sight, carried forward by the momentum of the radical programme and the military situation. The British were recruiting mercenaries from Germany and adding to their forces in Boston, but by the early spring of 1776 they had been forced to leave it, and the Americans had begun a dangerous invasion of Canada. In May Congress instructed the colonies to remove whatever traces were left of British administration, and they were replaced by revolutionary governments; in a fast-developing and inevitable two-way interaction, North Carolina, Virginia and Massachusetts instructed their delegates to vote for complete separation. In June, for the first time, the king was openly named as an enemy of the colonists, and the move towards republicanism had begun. The Declaration of Independence in July brought the colonists face to face with a situation that was almost alarming in its suddenness, for, with hardly a serious effort, they had rid themselves of nearly every vestige of British sovereignty.

PART FOUR

Assessment

ASSESSMENT

The future of an independent America had remained in the balance because there were still those who would have used the situation which had developed by 1776 to ask for no more than self-government within the empire. Their motives were mixed. Some still saw security and profit within the mercantile system; others were loth to wrench the branch off the parent tree and thus end the traditions of centuries, and perhaps saw in a continuing link with Britain a guarantee against radical upheaval at home; while still others faced without enthusiasm the dangers awaiting them in a new continent without the accustomed sanctions of British power, and with even less the consequences of waging war on that power itself.

The war resolved many of these doubts. The desire to withstand became the will to overcome; it could not be sustained with blurred aims or half-formed organisation, and the natural refining of both after 1776 signalled the arrival of a new nation. The support of European allies could not be relied on if the struggle was to lead to the reform rather than the destruction of the British Empire. Thus the achievement of independence became a positive aim; and Thomas Paine, then virtually unknown, brought the issue facing the American people to life in *Common Sense*, published in January 1776. This pamphlet sold 120,000 copies in the first week and gained what was probably the highest circulation of all revolutionary writing. In clear and rousing prose Paine poured scorn on the hesitations; the bonds in which the colonists had been held had worked to the advantage of Britain alone, and there was no chance of British victory or retaliation if the Americans acted quickly and decisively; and independence, once gained, could hold nothing but the most exciting of prospects [doc 26].

Yet to explain why the revolutionary process was fulfilled in a clear demand for total freedom rather than imperial adjustment, it is not enough to point to the activities of the demagogues and radical pamphleteers and journalists who carried the Congress of 1776 towards its crucial decision; nor to the growing national self-consciousness of a people at war; nor the need to match the war aims of the Americans with the powerful aspirations of future allies. These were but the last enlivening additions to be thrown among the raw ingredients of a controversy which stretched back over many years and which had been given its first tentative shape in the writings of moderates like Dulany and Dickinson as the Anglo-American crisis came to a head after 1763.

The question of the regulation of trade was never vital, for had there been a better relationship the British right to do so would have been willingly conceded. The issue of the western lands was more crucial, but it was the political and religious constitution of the new Canada, rather than its physical extent, which dominated the protests of the Declaration of Independence; and the problem of the frontier as a whole made little significant impression on the course of the dispute, save that it threw up the whole issue of taxation. But this by itself was of less importance than that, in the ineptness of its presentation, colonial leaders already steeped in the traditions of seventeenth-century resistance were given the chance to take an ideological stand on the issue that they would not suffer taxation at the hands of a body in which they were not represented. Since, however, few Americans really wanted actual representation, for it could never have been adequate and might well have opened the door to considerably more taxation, and totally rejected the notion that they were in some way virtually represented, they could do no more than advance the proposition that they should tax themselves.

The consequence was a clash of sovereignties which could not be resolved in eighteenth-century terms. Even Chatham's generosity could not prevent him from demanding colonial subordination in 1775, while Burke's glimpses of a lightly woven imperial structure of the future were imperfectly understood. Such federal solutions, like that of Galloway, could not be accepted by the unitary political thinking of the eighteenth century, and since all save that of Burke were expressed in a form involving some degree of royal supervision, it was precisely the more liberal minds of the age which found it most difficult to accept them. Yet their failures were small compared with those of the British ministers who found themselves responsible for the conduct of imperial affairs.

Revolutions are ultimately caused by the shortcomings of governments. In the case of America the failure was that of successive British ministries to achieve the reconstruction of the Anglo-American community that was so vital in the conditions of the second half of the eighteenth century, in a form that would attract the essential colonial consent. Here less blame lies with Grenville, whose policies were conceived with some imagination in face of very considerable imperial difficulties, than with Townshend, who, with the bitter experience of Grenville to guide him, embarked on a programme which contained little imperial vision and much petty provocation. Yet for all that, it was weakness in the execution of policy, not blind strength, which damned the English ministers; not tyranny, and certainly not royal tyranny, but a lack of consistency and purpose which allowed policies to be determined by the exigencies of political survival in an unstable domestic situation, and by the demands of powerful pressure groups. It was in this period of executive weakness that matters were allowed to drift to the point that moderate and reasonable protest in America turned into the anger which bred immoderate resistance; and when political stability was at last found in Britain after 1770 its essential expression had to come in a demand for an assertion of authority. Thus a failure to govern wisely produced extremism; the actions of demagogues in 1773 in America were met by the repressive Acts of 1774, and by the answer of men of equal desperation.

Thus there could be no going back, and no way forward save by an appeal to arms, and the coming of a war which extended the ministerial irresolution of earlier years and revealed the absence of the national preparedness which Grenville had been at pains to seek. The initial mistakes cost the early victory that some historians believe to have been possible; but it could only have been shortlived, for each month that followed brought the Americans, both in spirit and in form, nearer to the achievement of nationhood, and invited the foreign intervention which ensured that it would have to be fought to the bitter end. Saratoga, in 1778, brought a fearful realism to the North ministry, and with it the understanding that it would require 80,000 men at least to win the war, and a peace offering that would have granted all the demands of the First Continental Congress if the Americans had been prepared to resume their allegiance and accept Parliament's right to control their external trade. But it was too late; the Americans sensed success, for they had only to keep their armies in being to see the British challenge evaporate in the catastrophic loss of their command of the sea.

The empire was indeed at the crossroads, and Britain faced world-wide problems, in Ireland and India as well as in America, with a ministry weakened by resignations and a people slowly losing heart. The defeat at Yorktown spelt the end of North; the country gentlemen wavered, and the succeeding administration was filled with those who had always been identified with conciliation, and whose immediate object was to make peace. Only the king was more determined than his ministers and more resolute than his people; yet he remained only to represent that instinctive and unthinking British imperialism which was about to lose an empire because it could not produce administrations stable or imaginative enough to govern it wisely.

Shelburne came fully into his own. In charge of the peace negotiations when Rockingham died, he was by now completely convinced that the old concept of economic sovereignty was dead. A larger, freer America should join with an industrialised Britain in free commercial intercourse to create mutual prosperity. The Americans, as he had envisaged in 1767, would develop the wealth of the interior, and Britain would harness it to the developing economy of Europe. This, with imperfect understanding and unacceptable restraints, is what the politicians of the 1760s had been groping for, but it could be achieved only in free association.

The essential first step was a sensible peace, and he achieved it in partnership with his old friend, Franklin. The original American demand for Canada was dropped, for Franklin was prepared to concede it in order to get a separate, quicker and more generous settlement than one gained in association with continental allies whom he believed to be capable of neglecting the Americans in pursuit of their own ends. Shelburne was prepared to grant it, believing correctly that once the Americans had been satisfied they would not press the claims of their allies. Thus the colonists gained, if not Canada, a substantial frontier, a generous share of the interior and good commercial terms, concessions which seemed so great that Shelburne was reluctant to reveal to a sullen House the other and complementary side of his programme, that of a totally new commercial basis for the rest of the empire, to be built on free trade.

This, however, was the lesson of the whole American revolutionary crisis [doc. 28]. The loss of the colonies did not mean, as so many had feared, total ruin; because of a generous settlement with the Americans, Britain was able to go on to reconstruct her empire towards the end of free association, in the process of which the establishment of a better form of representative government in the Canadian territories, now full of loyalist refugees, was an essential step. Before long the Americans would be her best customers, and the two countries moved towards the profitable economic association which Shelburne had envisaged.

The process of breaking free of British control was bound to generate a greater degree of freedom in America. It is generally accepted that the radical pressure which did so much to launch the revolution had lost considerable momentum by the end of the war, and that the Federal and State constitutions which came after it were essentially conservative ones. In a movement, however, which had begun with fundamental and emotional declarations about the rights of man and democratic consent, it would be difficult for those who produced them to deny that they had validity inside America. The war, quite separately, brought a natural movement of social and political change. With, for example, the disappearance of the royal nominees, elected governors were established; their powers were reduced, limited generally by assemblies elected on a slightly wider franchise than before, if still representing something of an elite. It was a superior merchant group which still, by and large, managed the larger cities; and if the Revolution, at a low valuation, may be represented as an attempt to prevent the British Government from taxing wealth, and to increase the opportunities for the possession of land, then those who gained would be little inclined to share their power with those below. There was, in fact, a greater degree of representation generally for the back country, but for all these changes, the franchise remained a landed one.

Yet in the distribution of the land that supported the franchise there were significant changes, for the restrictions of the Proclamation and the Quebec Act had served to reinforce the existence of a privileged landowning group; now the frontier was fully and finally opened, and to a far greater number of people; crown possessions and loyalist estates were freely divided, and the abolition of primogeniture and the laws of entail in many of the states contributed to what appears to have been a more broadly based landowning and mercantile society. If there was no feudal order to be broken down, there was indeed a liberty to be enlarged. With the curtailment of the privileges of the established churches of the older settlers — for revolutionary leaders tended towards agnosticism — religious freedom was increased; public education, so essentially linked with the growth of democracy, began in New York in 1782 and spread slowly in the rest of the states, many of whom adopted bills of rights which would eventually find federal expression. Social change of the more immediate sort, however, was not obvious; there was little, either before or after the Revolution, to give adequate protection to the very poor, and while both Washington and Jefferson found slavery distasteful, no real effort was made towards emancipation; that awaited another war.

If some opening up of American society had been essential to the successful prosecution of the war it would also be the necessary prelude to a general effort to solve the enormous tasks faced by the new republic. A new unity, as well as a new liberty, had to be assured. Those who worked for a strong federal association were successful, and the problems faced by the American leadership after 1782 are, ironically and inevitably, those which so taxed the British statesmen who had earlier tried to create a new and more rigid pattern of empire. An interior remained to be developed, and for this a common degree of economic organisation had to be found; taxation had to provide the funds to support it, and decisions had to be taken about what each state should contribute to the federal authority and what it should be allowed to keep for itself. The American Revolution had merely decided the issue of which sovereign power was to be charged with the immense task of opening up a new continent. The problems which faced it remained the same, and had still to be resolved.

PART FIVE

Documents

Albany

The failure of the Albany Plan of Union of 1754, was predictable, but it is the earliest effective demonstration of the growing need for a comprehensive imperial policy.

July 10 1754

It is proposed that humble application be made for an Act of Parliament of Great Britain, by virtue of which one general government may be formed in America, including the said colonies, within and under which government each colony may retain its present constitution, except in the particulars wherein a change may be directed by the said act, as hereafter follows.

1. That the said general government be administered by a President-General, to be appointed and supported by the Crown; and a Grand Council, to be chosen by the representatives of the people of the several Colonies met in their respective assemblies . . .

10. That the President-General, with the advice of the Grand Council, hold or direct all Indian treaties, in which the general interest of the Colonies may be concerned; and make peace or declare war with Indian nations.

15. That they raise and pay soldiers and build forts for the defence of any of the Colonies, and equip vessels of force to guard the coasts and protect the trade on the ocean, lakes or great rivers; but they shall not impress men in any Colony, without the consent of the Legislature.

16. That for these purposes they have the power to make laws, and lay and levy such general duties, imposts, or taxes, as to them shall appear most equal and just (considering the

ability and other circumstances of the inhabitants in the several Colonies), and such as may be collected with the least inconvenience to the people; rather discouraging luxury, than loading industry with unnecessary burdens.

17. That they may appoint a General Treasurer and Particular Treasurer in each government when necessary; and, from time to time, may order the sums in the treasuries of each government into the general treasury; or draw on them for special payments, as they find most convenient.

Works of Benjamin Franklin, ed. Jared Sparks (1856), quoted in (9).

document 2

The Proclamation

The Proclamation of 1763 took British ministers a step nearer such a policy, and it was to become an essential part of the Grenville proposals; it differed radically from the Albany Plan, however, in that it contained no element of colonial volition or consent.

And whereas it is just and reasonable, and essential to our interest and the security of our colonies, that the several nations or tribes of Indians with whom we are connected, and who live under our protection, should not be molested or disturbed in the possession of such parts of our dominions and territories as, not having been ceded to or purchased by us, are reserved to them, or any of them, as their hunting-grounds; we do therefore, with the advice of our Privy Council, declare it to be our royal will and pleasure, that no Governor or commander in chief, in any of our colonies of Quebec, East Florida, or West Florida, do presume, upon any pretence whatever, to grant warrants of survey, or pass any patents for lands beyond the bounds of their respective governments, as described in their commissions; as also that no Governor or commander in chief of our other colonies or plantations in America do presume for the present, and until our further pleasure be known, to grant warrants of survey or pass patents for any lands beyond the heads or sources of any of the rivers which fall into the Atlantic Ocean from the west or north-west; or upon any lands whatever, which, not having been ceded to or purchased by us, as aforesaid, are reserved to the said Indians, or any of them.

And we do further declare it to be our royal will and pleasure, for the present as aforesaid, to reserve under our sovereignty, protection and dominion, for the use of the said Indians, all the land and territories not included within the limits of our said three new governments, or within the limits of the territory granted to the Hudson's Bay Company; as also all the land and territories lying to the westward of the sources of the rivers which fall into the sea from the west and north-west as aforesaid; and we do hereby strictly forbid, on pain of our displeasure, all our loving subjects from making any purchases or settlements whatever, or taking possession of any of the lands above reserved, without our special leave and licence for that purpose first obtained.

From the *Royal Proclamation on North America*, 7 October 1763, quoted in (**1**)

document 3

The Basis of Parliamentary Sovereignty

The assertion of sovereignty made here by Blackstone would have made Locke's ideas valid for the seventeenth century alone, and they provided the basis for the parliamentary imperialism which confronted the Americans after 1763.

It must be owned that Mr Locke, and other theoretical writers, have held that 'there remains still inherent in the people a supreme power to remove or alter the legislative, when they find the legislative act contrary to the trust reposed in them: for when such trust is abused, it is thereby forfeited, and devolves to those who have it.' But however just this conclusion may be in theory, we cannot adopt it, nor argue from it, under any dispensation of government at present actually existing. For this devolution of power, to the people at large, includes in it a dissolution of the whole form of government established by that people, reduces all the members to their original state of equality and by annihilating the sovereign power repeals all positive laws whatsoever before enacted. No human laws will therefore suppose a case, which at once must destroy all law, and compel men to build afresh upon a new foundation; nor will they make provision for so desperate an event, as must render all legal provisions ineffectual. So long therefore as the English constitution lasts, we may venture to affirm, that the power of parliament is absolute and without control.

From William Blackstone, *Commentaries on the Laws of England*, 1765-69, quoted in (3).

document 4

James Otis on the British Constitution

Otis here seeks to qualify this power. The hyperbole is not untypical of the early 1760s, for the Americans of the time generally worshipped the British Constitution, and Otis sought no more than representation; yet there is also an interesting and early suggestion of the divine or natural law that the colonists had in the end to appeal to in order to assert their rights against a sovereign parliament.

To say the Parliament is absolute and arbitrary is a contradiction. The Parliament cannot make 2 and 2, 5: Omnipotency cannot do it. . . . Parliaments are in all cases to declare what is for the good of the whole; but it is not the declaration of Parliament that makes it so: There must be in every instance a higher authority, viz. God. Should an Act of Parliament be against any of His natural laws, which are immutably true, their declaration would be contrary to eternal truth, equity, and justice, and consequently void: and so it would be adjudged by the Parliament itself, when convinced of their mistake. . . . See here the grandeur of the British constitution! See the wisdom of our ancestors! The supreme legislative and the supreme executive, are a perpetual check and balance to each other. If the supreme executive errs, it is informed by the supreme legislative in Parliament: if the supreme legislative errs, it is informed by the supreme executive in the King's courts of law. Here, the King appears, as represented by his judges, in the highest lustre and majesty, as supreme executor of the Commonwealth; and he never shines brighter, but on his throne, at the head of the supreme legislative.

James Otis, *The Rights of the British Colonies asserted and proved,* Boston, 1764, quoted in (1).

document 5

The Sugar Act

Otis was in fact one of the first American publicists to discern the significance of the Sugar Act of 1764, about which he wrote. Here, however, is the first official sign that the duties which regulated trade, and which were as such generally acceptable, could be used as a source of quite intentional revenue.

Whereas it is expedient that new provisions and regulations should be established for improving the revenue of this kingdom, and for extending and securing the navigation and commerce between Great Britain and your Majesty's dominions in America, which, by the peace, have been so happily enlarged: and whereas it is just and necessary, that a revenue be raised, in your Majesty's said dominions in America, for defraying the expences of defending, protecting and securing the same; we, your Majesty's most dutiful and loyal subjects, the commons of Great Britain, in parliament assembled, being desirous to make some provision, in this present session of parliament, towards raising the said revenue in America, have resolved to give and grant unto your Majesty the several rates and duties herein aftermentioned . . .

From the *Preamble to the Sugar Act,* 4 George III, c. 15, quoted in (4).

document 6

The Colonial Position at the end of 1764

The Virginia Petitions to the King and Parliament of 18 December 1764, were not only concerned to protest at the implications of the

Sugar Act. Grenville, in introducing it, had mentioned the possibility of direct taxation, and the Virginians were at pains to emphasise the constitutional position they believed to have emerged by the middle of the eighteenth century and the more immediate reasons why they should not be taxed.

Your Memorialists have been invested with the Right of taxing their own People from the first Establishment of a regular Government in the Colony, and Requisitions have been constantly made to them by their Sovereigns on all Occasions when the Assistance of the Colony was thought necessary to preserve the *British* Interest in America; from whence they must conclude they cannot now be deprived of a Right they have so long enjoyed, and which they have never forfeited.

The Expenses incurred during the last War, in Compliance with the Demands on this Colony by our late and present most gracious Sovereigns, have involved us in a Debt of near Half a Million; a Debt not likely to decrease under the continued Expense we are at in providing for the Security of the People against the Incursions of our savage Neighbours, at a Time when the low state of our Staple Commodity, the total Want of Specie, and the late Restrictions on the Trade of the Colonies, render the Circumstances of the People extremely distressful, and which, if Taxes are accumulated upon them by the *British* Parliament, will make them truly deplorable.

Journals of the House of Burgesses of Virginia, 1761-5, ed. Kennedy, quoted in **(4)**.

document 7

The Prelude to the Stamp Act

Thomas Whately, Secretary to the Treasury under Grenville, in dismissing colonial objections, set out the basis of the right to tax.

The Concurrence, therefore, of the provincial Representatives cannot be necessary in great public Measures to which none but the national Representatives are equal: the Parliament of *Great Britain* not only may but must tax the Colonies, when the public Occasions require a Revenue there: the present

Circumstances of the Nation require one now; and a Stamp Act, of which we have had so long an Experience in this, and which is not unknown in that Country, seems an eligible Mode of Taxation. From all these Considerations, and from many others which will occur upon Reflexion and need not be suggested, it must appear *proper to charge certain Stamp Duties in the Plantations to be applied towards defraying the necessary Expences of defending, protecting and securing the British Colonies and Plantations in America.*

Thomas Whately, *The Regulations lately Made concerning the Colonies and the Taxes Imposed upon Them Considered,* London, 1765, quoted in (4).

document 8

The Stamp Act Congress

The Congress distilled colonial resentment in October 1765, and their claim to be able to tax themselves had inevitably to lead to the demand for equal sovereignty.

The members of this Congress, sincerely devoted with the warmest sentiments of affection and duty to His Majesty's person and Government, inviolably attached to the present happy establishment of the Protestant succession, and with minds deeply impressed by a sense of the present and impending misfortunes of the British colonies on this continent; having considered as maturely as time will permit the circumstances of the said colonies, esteem it our indispensable duty to make the following declarations of our humble opinion respecting the most essential rights and liberties of the colonists, and of the grievances under which they labour, by reason of several late Acts of Parliament.

I. That His Majesty's subjects in these colonies owe the same allegiance to the Crown of Great Britain that is owing from his subjects born within the realm, and all due subordination to that august body the Parliament of Great Britain.

II. That His Majesty's liege subjects in these colonies are intitled to all the inherent rights and liberties of his natural born subjects within the kingdom of Great Britain.

III. That it is inseparably essential to the freedom of a people, and the undoubted right of Englishmen, that no taxes be imposed on them but with their own consent, given personally or by their representatives.

IV. That the people of these colonies are not, and from their local circumstances cannot be, represented in the House of Commons in Great Britain.

V. That the only representatives of the people of these colonies are persons chosen therein by themselves, and that no taxes ever have been, or can be constitutionally imposed on them, but by their respective legislatures.

Resolutions of the Stamp Act Congress, quoted in (1).

document 9

Direct and Indirect Taxation

The question at issue here is whether the Americans, having refused to accept the principle of direct taxation, could be induced to see indirect taxation in a different light. Certainly a restrained petition from the delegates to the Stamp Act Congress had suggested that some distinction might be made between the internal and external authority of Parliament. But this was not quite the same thing, and Dulany and Pitt are quite clear on the view that the Americans would eventually take up; but Franklin's evasions made it possible for the Repeal of the Stamp Act to be carried more effectively, and gave some justification for the Townshend Revenue Act of 1767.

[a] It appears to me that there is a clear and necessary Distinction between an Act imposing a tax for *the single purpose of revenue,* and those Acts which have been made for the *regulation of trade,* and have produced some revenue in consequence of their effect and operation as regulations of trade.

Daniel Dulany, *Considerations on the Propriety of imposing Taxes in the British Colonies, for the purpose of Raising a Revenue, by Act of Parliament,* Annapolis, 1765, quoted in (1).

[b] If the gentleman does not understand the difference between external and internal taxes, I cannot help it; but there

is a plain distinction between taxes levied for the purposes of raising a revenue, and duties imposed for the regulation of trade, for the accommodation of the subject; although in the consequences, some revenue might incidentally arise from the latter.

William Pitt, in the House of Commons, 14 January 1766, quoted in (3).

[c] Q. You say the colonies have always submitted to external taxes, and object to the right of parliament only in laying internal taxes; now can you show that there is any kind of difference between the two taxes to the colony on which they may be laid?

A. I think the difference is very great. An external tax is a duty laid on commodities imported; that duty is added to the first cost, and other charges on the commodity, and when it is offered to sale, makes a part of the price. If the people do not like it at that price, they refuse it; they are not obliged to pay it. But an internal tax is forced from the people without their consent, if not laid by their own representatives.

From Benjamin Franklin's Examination before Parliament, 1766, in W. Cobbett's *The Parliamentary History of England,* vol. XVI, quoted in (3).

document 10

Virtual Representation

Another possible way out of the deadlock over taxation was for the Americans to accept that they were indirectly represented in the British Parliament. They would not, and were led not only to demand legislative competence for themselves, but to go on to make their own system of representation more precise.

I am well aware that I shall hear Lock [*sic*], Sidney, Selden, and many other great names quoted to prove that every Englishman, whether he has a right to vote for a representative or not, is still represented in the British Parliament, in which opinion they all agree. On what principle of common sense this is founded I comprehend not, but on the authority of such respectable names I shall acknowledge its truth; but then I will ask one question, and on that I will rest the whole merits of the case. Why does not this imaginary representation extend to America as well as over the whole Island of Great Britain? If it can travel three hundred miles, why not three thousand? If it can jump over rivers and mountains, why cannot it sail over the ocean? If the towns of Manchester and Birmingham, sending no representatives to Parliament, are notwithstanding there represented, why are not the cities of Albany and Boston equally represented in that Assembly? Are they not alike British subjects? are they not Englishmen? or are they only Englishmen when they sollicit for protection, but not Englishmen when taxes are required to enable this country to protect them?

Soame Jenyns, *The Objections to the Taxation of our American Colonies by the Legislature of Great Britain, briefly consider'd,* London, 1765, quoted in (1).

document 11

The Repeal of the Stamp Act

Camden here restates the original Whiggism which motivated the small number of friends of America. Bernard, on the other hand, pursues the logic of repeal to its inevitable conclusion.

[a] 'The supreme power cannot take from any man part of his property, without his consent.' Such are the words of this great man, and which are well worth your serious attention. His principles are drawn from the heart of our constitution, which he thoroughly understood, and will last as long as that shall last; and, to his immortal honour, I know not to what, under providence, the Revolution and all its happy effects, are more owing, than to the principles of government laid down by Mr Locke. For these reasons, my lords, I can never give my assent to any bill for taxing the American colonies, while they remain unrepresented; for as to the distinction of virtual representation, it is so absurd as not to deserve an answer; I therefore pass it over with contempt.

Lord Camden, in the debate in the House of Lords on the Repeal of the

Stamp Act, 24 February 1766, in Cobbett's *Parliamentary History*, vol. XVI, quoted in (6).

[b] The Stamp Act is become in itself a matter of indifference; it is swallowed up in the importance of the effects of which it has been the cause. The taxing of the Americans by the Parliament, has brought their very subjection to the Crown of Great Britain in question . . . the people [of America] have felt their strength, and flatter themselves that it is much greater than it is; and will not, of their own accord, submit readily to anything they do not like: and there is no internal principle of policy which can by any means restore the power of Government, and enforce a due subordination . . . February 28, 1766.

From Sir Francis Bernard, Governor of Massachusetts, 1760-69, *Select Letters on the Trade and Government of America*, 1774, quoted in (3).

document 12

The Frontier Question

An Indian account of the frontier issues which were to play such an important part in the formulation of western policy, even if, in practice, it was often evaded.

We have often put you in mind of the many promises which were made to us at the beginning of the late war by the Generals, Governors, and by yourself, from all which we had the strongest reason to expect that the event of your success would have proved greatly to our benefit. . . . At the same time the French told us that what you said was not true, not from your hearts; and that the day you got the better of them would be the first day of our misfortunes. You persuaded us not to believe them, but we have found it since too true. We soon found ourselves ill used at the posts, on the frontiers, and by the traders. . . . The rum bottles hung at every door to steal our lands, and instead of the English protecting us as we thought they would do, they employed their superior cunning to wrong us, they murdered our people in Pensilvania [*sic*], Virginia, and all over the country, and the traders began more and more to deceive, and now neither regard their own character, or the officers sent to take care of the trade, so that if we are wronged, who is to help us? We cant ramble over the country for justice, and if we did, we begin now to grow old and wise, we see your wise men in the towns will be always against us. Your people come from the sun, rising up our rivers to the west, and now they begin to come upon us from the south, they have got already almost to Fort Pitt, but nothing is done to drive them away.

Proceedings of a General Congress of the Chiefs of the Indian tribes with Sir William Johnson, March 1768, Public Record Office, London, C.O. 5, 69, pp. 329-48, quoted in (1).

document 13

The Death of the Shelburne Plan

The Board of Trade Report of 1768 killed the imaginative Shelburne proposals of 1767 which might well have brought peace to the frontier; it emphasises the still strong influence of mercantilism upon the making of official policy.

The proposition of forming inland colonies in America is, we humbly conceive, entirely new; it adopts principles in respect to American settlements different from what has hitherto been the policy of this kingdom; and leads to a system which, if pursued through all its consequences, is in the present state of this country of the greatest importance.

The great object of colonizing upon the Continent of North America has been to improve and extend the commerce, navigation and manufactures of this kingdom, upon which its strength and security depend: (1) by promoting the advantageous fishery carried on upon the northern coast; (2) by encouraging the growth and culture of naval stores, and of raw materials to be transported hither in exchange for perfect manufacture and other merchandise; (3) by securing a supply of lumber, provisions and other necessaries for the support of our establishments in the American islands.

In order to answer these salutary purposes it has been the policy of this Kingdom to confine her settlements as much as possible to the sea coast and not to extend them to places un-accessible to shipping and consequently more out of the reach of commerce, a plan which at the same time . . . had the further political advantage of guarding against all inter-fering of foreign powers and of enabling this Kingdom to keep up a superior naval force in those seas, by the actual possession of such rivers and harbours as were proper stations for fleets in time of war. . . .

From the Report of the Board of Trade and Plantations on the Western Problem, 7 March 1768, Public Record Office, C.O. 5, 69, quoted in (1).

document 14

The Townshend Duties

The effect of the Revenue Act of 1767 was far more than in its bringing to an end the attempt to make a valid distinction between internal and external authority, for the first doubts about this had been sown in the preamble to the Sugar Act of 1764. It posed a constitutional threat to which American patriot leaders were particularly sensitive.

That from and after the twentieth day of November, one thousand seven hundred and sixty seven, there shall be raised, levied, collected, and paid unto his Majesty, his heirs, and successors, for and upon the respective goods herein after mentioned, which shall be imported from Great Britain into any colony or plantation in America which now is, or here-after may be, under the dominion of his Majesty, his heirs, or successors, the several rates and duties following . . . and that all the monies that shall arise by the said duties . . . shall be applied in the first place, in such a manner as is herein after mentioned, in making a more certain and adequate provision for the charge of the administration of justice, and the sup-port of civil government, in such of the said colonies and plantations where it shall be found necessary.

From *The Statutes at Large*, ed. Danby Pickering, Cambridge, 1762-1807, quoted in (3).

John Dickinson's Reply

Dickinson saw the constitutional dangers in the Act, and exposed them clearly. His pamphlets were the most influential of all pre-revolutionary writings.

The consequences, mentioned in the last letter, will not be the utmost limits of our misery and infamy, if the late Act is acknowledged to be binding upon us. We feel, too sensibly, that any ministerial measures relating to these colonies, are soon carried successfully through the Parliament. Certain prejudices operate there so strong against us that it may be justly questioned whether all the provinces united will ever be able effectually to call to an account before the Parliament any minister who shall abuse the power by the late Act given to the Crown in America. He may divide the spoils torn from us in what manner he pleases, and we shall have no way of making him responsible. If he should order that every Governor shall have a yearly salary of 5,000*l* sterling; every chief Justice of 3,000*l*; every inferior officer in proportion; and should then reward the most profligate, ignorant, or needy dependents on himself or his friends with places of the greatest trust, because they were of the greatest profit, this would be called an arrangement in consequence of the 'adequate provision for defraying the charge of the administration of justice and the support of the civil government'. And if the taxes should prove at any time insufficient to answer all the expences of the numberless offices which ministers may please to create, surely the members of the House of Commons will be so 'modest' as not to 'contradict a minister' who shall tell them it is become necessary to lay a new tax upon the colonies for the laudable purposes of defraying the charges of the 'administration of justice and support of civil government' among them. Thus, in fact, we shall be taxed by ministers. In short, it will be in their power to settle upon us any civil, ecclesiastical, or military establishment which they choose.

John Dickinson, *Letters from a Farmer in Pennsylvania to the Inhabitants of the British Colonies,* Philadelphia, 1768, Letter 10, quoted in (1).

Proceedings of the Boston Town Meeting 1772

The fears expressed by Dickinson were not completely allayed by the repeal of the bulk of the Townshend duties. That on tea remained, and by 1772 a not inconsiderable sum was being collected through indirect parliamentary taxation. Samuel Adams and his fellow radicals felt that it was time to rouse their fellow Bostonians from what seemed to be a mood of dangerous acquiescence.

The Revenue arising from this tax unconstitutionally laid, and committed to the management of persons arbitrarily appointed and supported by an armed force quartered in a free city, has been in part applyed to the most destructive purposes. It is absolutely necessary in a mixt government like that of this Province, that a due proportion or balance of power should be established among the several branches of the legislative. Our ancestors received from King William and Queen Mary a charter by which it was understood by both parties in the contract, that such a proportion or balance was fixed; and therefore everything which renders any one branch of the legislative more independent of the other two than it was originally designed, is an alteration of the constitution as settled by the charter; and as it has been untill the establishment of this revenue, the constant practise of the General Assembly to provide for the support of government, so it is an essential part of our constitution, as it is a necessary means of preserving an equilibrium, without which we cannot continue a free state.

The Sixth Point from the List of Infringements and Violations of Rights prepared by the Committee of Correspondence set up by the Boston Town Meeting in November 1772, quoted in (1).

Repression

Radical political activity in Boston culminated in the Boston Tea Party of 1773 and the Massachusetts Government Act of 1774. The latter, far from merely tilting the balance of the constitution in favour of the

executive, suspended the whole machinery of representative govern-
ment and inaugurated the repressive policies that were to take the
Anglo-American conflict into a new field.

(Whereas, the method of electing the Councillors of this Province, under the Charter of 1691), hath, for some time past
been such as had the most manifest tendency to obstruct,
and in great measure defeat the execution of the laws; to
weaken the attachment of His Majesty's well-disposed subjects in the said Province to His Majesty's government, and to
encourage the ill-disposed among them to proceed even to
acts of direct resistance to and defiance of His Majesty's
authority. . . . Be it therefore enacted (that so much of the
said Charter which relates to the election of Councillors) is
hereby revoked . . . (and that from 1 August 1774) the Council, or Court of Assistants of the said Province for the time
being, shall be composed of such of the inhabitants or proprietors of lands within the same as shall be thereunto nominated and appointed by His Majesty, his heirs and successors,
from time to time, by warrant under his or their signet or
sign manual, and with the advice of the Privy Council, agree-
able to the practice now used in respect to the appointment
of Counsellors in such of His Majesty's other colonies in
America, the Governors whereof are appointed by commission under the great seal of Great Britain. . . .

From the Massachusetts Government Act, 14 Geo III, c. 45, quoted in
(1).

document 18

Burke and Chatham in 1774

Both appealed in vain for understanding and conciliation. Chatham
rightly condemned the total punishment of the Acts of 1774, but the
Americans were reaching a maturity of outlook which was already in-
validating the image of the erring child. Burke still did not question
the authority of Parliament, but in relation to the empire saw it as
wise guide and mentor, a reserve power in case of colonial insuffi-
ciency.

[a] By blocking up the harbour of Boston, you have involved
the innocent trader in the same punishment with the guilty pro-

fligates who destroyed your merchandize; and instead of making a concerted effort to secure the real offenders, you clap a naval and military extinguisher over their harbour, and punish the crime of a few lawless depredators and their abettors upon the whole body of the inhabitants. . . .

This, my Lords, though no new doctrine, has always been my received and unalterable opinion, and I will carry it to my grave, *that this country had no right under heaven to tax America.* It is contrary to all the principles of justice and civil policy, which neither the exigencies of the state, nor even an acquiescence in the taxes, could justify upon any occasion whatever. Such proceedings will never meet their wished-for success; and instead of adding to their miseries, as the bill now before you most undoubtedly does, adopt some lenient measures, which may lure them to their duty; proceed like a kind and affectionate parent over a child whom he tenderly loves; and instead of those harsh and severe proceedings, pass an amnesty on all their youthful errors; clasp them once more in your fond and affectionate arms; and I will venture to affirm you will find them children worthy of their sire.

From Chatham's speech on the third reading of the Massachusetts Government Bill in the House of Lords, 26 May 1774, quoted in **(6)**.

[b] What is to become of the declaratory act asserting the entireness of British legislative authority, if we abandon the practice of taxation?

For my part I look upon the rights stated in that act, exactly in the manner in which I viewed them on its very first proposition, and which I have often taken the liberty, with great humility, to lay before you. I look, I say, on the imperial rights of Great Britain, and the privileges which the colonists ought to enjoy under these rights, to be just the most reconcileable things in the world. The parliament of Great Britain fits at the head of her extensive empire in two capacities: one as the local legislature of this island, providing for all things at home, immediately, and by no other instrument than the executive power. — The other, and I think her nobler capacity, is what I call her *imperial character*; in which, as from the throne of heaven, she superintends all the several inferiour legislatures, and guides, and controuls them all without annihilating any. As all these provincial legislatures are only co-ordinate to each other, they ought all to be subordinate to her; else they can neither preserve mutual peace, nor hope for mutual justice, nor effectually afford mutual assistance. It is necessary to coerce the negligent, to restrain the violent, and to aid the weak and deficient, by the over-ruling plenitude of her power. She is never to intrude into the place of the others, whilst they are equal to the common ends of their institution. But in order to enable parliament to answer all these ends of provident and beneficent superintendance, her powers must be boundless.

. . . Such, Sir, is my idea of the constitution of the British empire, as distinguished from the constitution of Britain; and on these grounds I think subordination and liberty may be sufficiently reconciled through the whole; whether to serve a refining speculatist, or a factious demagogue, I know not; but surely enough for the ease and happiness of man.

Edmund Burke, Speech on American Taxation, House of Commons, 19 April 1774, quoted in (6).

document 19

James Wilson

Burke's reluctance to surrender the sovereignty of parliament established a fundamental barrier between him and the colonial radicals – indeed, his injunction to the Americans that they should tax themselves or be taxed differs little from North's offer of conciliation of February 1775. For influential writers like Wilson were about to deny the authority of Parliament in every sense; even the regulation of trade, as he here suggests, should lie in a mutual, even contractual, identity of interest. The passage also marks an appreciation of the free trade doctrines that were to transform Britain's overseas and imperial position.

After considering, with all the attention of which I am capable, the foregoing opinion – that all the different members of the British empire are distinct states, independent of each other, but connected together under the same sovereign in right of the same Crown – I discover only one objection that can be offered against it . . . 'How, it will be urged, can the trade of the British Empire be carried on, without some power, extending over the whole, to regulate it?'

. . . It has been the opinion of some politicians, of no inferior note, that all regulations of trade are useless; that the greatest part of them are hurtful; and that the stream of commerce never flows with so much beauty and advantage, as when it is not diverted from its natural channels. Whether this opinion is well founded or not, let others determine. Thus much may certainly be said, that commerce is not so properly the object of laws, as of treaties and compacts.

James Wilson, *Considerations on the Nature and Extent of the Legislative Authority of the British Parliament*, Philadelphia, 1774, quoted in (1).

document 20

Thomas Jefferson

Jefferson also denied the authority of Parliament, and he, too, appealed to the king for justice; and for the first time a writer of stature, for the pamphlet made Jefferson's national reputation, suggests that American rights rested upon natural law.

That these are our grievances, which we have thus laid before his Majesty, with that freedom of language and sentiment which becomes a free people, claiming their rights as derived from the laws of nature, and not as the gift of their Chief Magistrate. Let those flatter, who fear: it is not an American art. To give praise where it is not due might be well from the venal, but would ill beseem those who are asserting the rights of human nature. They know, and will, therefore, say, that Kings are the servants, not the proprietors of the people.

Thomas Jefferson, *A Summary View of the Rights of British America*, from *The Complete Jefferson*, New York, 1943, quoted in (6).

First Continental Congress 1774

The Declaration and Resolves of the First Congress were the result of compromise between radical and conservative delegates; while there is an obvious wish to return to the conditions that were supposed to have existed before the Seven Years War, the tone of some of the resolves would make retreat difficult.

Whereupon the deputies so appointed being now assembled, in a full and free representation of these colonies, taking into their most serious consideration the best means of attaining the ends aforesaid, do in the first place, as Englishmen their ancestors in like cases have usually done, for asserting and vindicating their rights and liberties, *declare,*

That the inhabitants of the English colonies in North America, by the immutable laws of nature, the principles of the English Constitution, and the several charters or compacts, have the following rights:

1. That they are entitled to life, liberty, and property, and they have never ceded to any sovereign power whatever, a right to dispose of either without their consent . . .

4. That the foundation of English liberty, and of all free government, is a right in their people to participate in their legislative council: and as the English colonists are not represented, and from their local and other circumstances, cannot properly be represented in the British Parliament, they are entitled to a free and exclusive power of legislation in their several provincial legislatures, where their right of representation can alone be preserved, in all cases of taxation and internal polity. . . . But, from the necessity of the case, and a regard to the mutual interest of both countries, we cheerfully consent to the operation of such Acts of the British Parliament, as are bona fide restrained to the regulation of our external commerce, for the purpose of securing the commercial advantages of the whole empire to the mother country, and the commercial benefits of its respective members; excluding every idea of taxation, internal or external, for raising a revenue on the subjects in America without their consent . . .

9. That the keeping of a standing army in these colonies,

in times of peace, without the consent of the legislature of that colony in which such army is kept, is against the law.

10. It is indispensably necessary to good government, and rendered essential by the English Constitution, that the constituent branches of the legislature be independent of each other; that, therefore, the exercise of legislative power in several colonies, by a council appointed during pleasure, by the Crown, is unconstitutional, dangerous, and destructive to the freedom of American legislation.

Declaration and Resolves of the First Continental Congress, quoted in (1).

document 22

The Suffolk County Resolves

The County of Suffolk, which contained Boston, had decided to disobey the coercive Acts, and sought the help of Massachusetts and the other colonies. The position it had taken up was that there was no general obligation to obey them, and when Congress adopted their resolutions it was really insisting that there could be no conciliation without their repeal, and, in a sense, giving its sanction to the resistance which had already taken place in Boston.

Resolved unanimously, That this assembly ... most thoroughly approve the wisdom and fortitude, with which opposition to these wicked ministerial measures has hitherto been conducted, and they earnestly recommend to their brethren, a perseverance in the same firm and temperate conduct as expressed in the resolutions determined upon ... trusting that the effect of the united efforts of North America in their behalf, will carry such convictions to the British nation, of the unwise, unjust, and ruinous policy of the present administration, as quickly to introduce better men and wiser measures.

From the Journals of the Continental Congress, quoted in Oscar Handlin, *The History of the United States,* vol. 1, Holt, Rinehart and Winston, 1967.

Novanglus

*The feelings expressed here were widely held in America by the begin-
ning of 1775. By then the authority of Parliament was generally denied;
but a return to a relationship which had existed only on neglect, or an
advance to a freer association under royal supervision, was virtually
impossible in the conditions of the time.*

There is no avoiding all inconveniences in human affairs. The
greatest possible, or conceivable, would arise from ceding to
Parliament power over us without a representation in it. The
next greatest would accrue from any plan that can be devised
for a representation there. The least of all would arise from
going on as we began, and fared well for one hundred and
fifty years, by letting Parliament regulate trade, and our own
assemblies all other matters.

We are a part of the British dominions, that is, of the King
of Great Britain, and it is our interest and duty to continue
so. It is equally our interest and duty to continue subject to
the authority of Parliament in the regulation of our trade, as
long as she shall leave us to govern our internal policy, and
give and grant our own money, and no longer.

John Adams, *Novanglus, No. VII,* from *The Works of John Adams,*
1851, quoted in (1).

Towards Independence

*As the year wore on, American enthusiasm for a continued association
with Britain, even on the terms of Wilson or Adams, seemed to wane.
Franklin, informing Galloway of the British repudiation of the Plan of
Union which had been so narrowly defeated by the First Congress,
seems to reject entirely any connection with a decadent nation, and
pours scorn on Lord North's tepid proposals of conciliation. In the next
extract, Joseph Warren, writing to Arthur Lee, exudes a confidence in
America's destiny to create a new freedom which is almost a call to
arms.*

I have not heard what objections were made to the plan in the Congress, nor would I make more than this one, that, when I consider the extreme corruption prevalent among all orders of men in this old, rotten state, and the glorious public virtue so predominant in our rising country, I cannot but apprehend more mischief than benefit from a closer union.

... It seems like Mezentius' coupling and binding together the dead and the living ...

... You will see the new proposal of Lord North, made on Monday last, which I have sent to the committee. Those in administration, who are for violent measures, are said to dislike it. The other rely upon it as a means of dividing, and by that means subduing us. But I cannot conceive that any colony will undertake to grant a revenue to a government that holds a sword over their heads with a threat to strike the moment they cease to give or do not give so much as it is pleased to expect. In such a situation, where is the right of giving our own property freely or the right to judge of our own ability to give? It seems to me the language of a highwayman who, with a pistol in your face says: 'Give me your purse, and then I will not put my hand into your pocket. But give me all your money, or I will shoot you through the head.'

Benjamin Franklin to Joseph Galloway, 25 February, 1775, quoted in (1).

document 25

Joseph Warren to Arthur Lee

Boston, 3 April 1775
... If we ever obtain a redress of grievances from Great Britain, it must be under the influence of those illustrious personages whose virtue now keeps them out of power. The King never will bring them into power until the ignorance and frenzy of the present administration make the throne on which he sits shake under him. If America is an humble in-

strument of the salvation of Britain, it will give us the sincerest joy; but, if Britain must lose her liberty, she must lose it alone. America must and will be free. The contest may be severe; the end will be glorious . . .

From Richard Frothingham, *Life of Joseph Warren*, 1865, quoted in (1).

document 26

Common Sense

In spite of the strictures of Franklin and Warren on the mother country, it was, ironically, an English radical who presented independence to the Americans as an exciting prospect. Paine maintained, in January 1776, that a declaration of independence had become a matter of urgency.

To conclude, however strange it may appear to some, or however unwilling they may be to think so, matters not, but many strong, and striking reasons may be given, to shew, that nothing can settle our affairs so expeditiously as an open, and determined declaration for independence. Some of which are,

First. It is the custom of nations, when any two are at war, for some other powers, not engaged in the quarrel, to step in as mediators, and bring about the preliminaries of a peace: but while America calls herself the subject of Great Britain, no power, however well disposed she may be, can offer her mediation. Wherefore, in our present state we may quarrel on for ever.

Secondly. It is unreasonable to suppose, that France or Spain will give us any kind of assistance, if we mean only to make use of that assistance for the purpose of repairing the breach, and strengthening the connexion between Britain, and America; because, those powers would be sufferers by the consequences.

Thirdly. While we profess ourselves the subjects of Britain, we must, in the eye of foreign nations, be considered as rebels. The precedent is somewhat dangerous to *their peace*, for men to be in arms under the name of subjects; we, on the spot, can solve the paradox: but to unite resistance, and subjection, requires an idea much too refined for common undertaking.

Fourthly. Were a manifesto to be published, and dispatched to foreign courts, setting forth the miseries we have endured, and the peaceable methods we have ineffectually used for redress; declaring at the same time, that not being able, any longer, to live happily or safely under the cruel disposition of the British court, we had been driven to the necessity of breaking off all connexion with her; at the same time assuring all such courts of our peaceable disposition towards them, and of our desire of entering into trade with them: such a memorial would produce more good effects to this Continent, than if a ship were freighted with petitions to Britain.

Under our present denomination of British subjects, we can neither be received nor heard abroad: The custom of all courts is against us, and will be so, until, by an independence, we take rank with other nations.

[Appendix to the second edition]
The birth-day of a new world is at hand, and a race of men perhaps as numerous as all Europe contains, are to receive their portion of freedom from the events of a few months. The reflexion is awful — and in this point of view, how trifling, how ridiculous, do the little paltry cavillings, of a few weak, or interested men appear, when weighed against the business of a world.

Thomas Paine, *Common Sense,* Philadelphia, January 1776, quoted in (6).

document 27

The Determination of the King

The king, in exhorting his ministers to be firm and hold to the Empire, permits himself but one wry observation of regret.

The present Contest with America I cannot help seeing as the most serious in which any Country was ever engaged it contains such a train of consequences that they must be examined to feel its real weight; whether the laying of a Tax was deserving all the Evile that have arisen from it, I should suppose no man could alledge that without being thought more fit for Bedlam than a Seat in the Senate; but step by step the demands of America have arisen – independence is their object, that certainly is one which every man not willing to sacrifice every object to a *momentary and* inglorious Peace must concurr with me in thinking that this Country can never submit to; should America succeed in that, the West Indies must follow them, not independence, but must for its own interest be dependent on North America; Ireland would soon follow the same plan and be a separate State, then this Island would be reduced to itself, and soon would be a poor Island indeed, for reduced in Her Trade Merchants would retire with their wealth to Climates more to their Advantage, and Shoals of Manufacturers would leave this country for the New Empire; these self-evident consequences, are not worse than what can arise should the Almighty permit every event to turn out to our disadvantage; consequently this Country has but one Sensible, one great line to follow, the being ever ready to make Peace when to be obtained without submitting to terms that in their consequence must annihilate this Empire, and with firmness to make every effort to deserve Success.

The King to Lord North, 11 June 1779, quoted in (3).

document 28

Adam Smith

Already, however, the end of the old empire had been signalled; the wealth of the nineteenth century, contrary to the fears of the king, would not depend upon the outright possession of colonial territories.

The rulers of Great Britain have, for more than a century past, amused the people with the imagination that they possessed a great empire on the west side of the Atlantic. It is surely now time that our rulers should either realize this golden dream, in which they have been indulging themselves, perhaps, as well as the people; or, that they should awake from it themselves and endeavour to awaken the people. If the project cannot be completed, it ought to be given up. If any of the provinces of the British empire cannot be made to contribute towards the support of the whole empire, it is surely time that Great Britain should free herself from the expence of defending those provinces in time of war, and of supporting any part of their civil or military establishments in time of peace, and endeavour to accommodate her future views and designs to the real mediocrity of her circumstances.

Adam Smith, *An Inquiry into the Nature and Causes of the Wealth of Nations*, 1776, quoted in (**3**).

document 29

A Final Comment

I have the comfort of seeing that America may be free if it will. It is the only country that ever had an opportunity of choosing its constitution at once; it may take the best one that ever was, ours, and correct its defects.

Horace Walpole to the Rev. William Mason, 21 March 1782, from *The Letters of Horace Walpole,* Oxford, 1903, quoted in (**3**).

Bibliography

COLLECTIONS OF ORIGINAL MATERIAL

1. Morison, S.E. ed. *Sources and Documents Illustrating the American Revolution,* paperback, Oxford University Press, 1965.
2. Commager, Henry S., *Documents of American History,* Appleton-Century-Crofts, 1958.
3. Kallich, Martin and Macleish, Andrew, *The American Revolution through British Eyes,* Harper, 1962.
4. Morgan, Edmund S., ed. *Prologue to Revolution, 1764-66,* North Carolina University Press, repr. Norton, 1972.
5. Bailyn, Bernard, ed. *Pamphlets of the American Revolution,* vol. 1, Harvard University Press, 1965.
6. Beloff, Max, ed. *The Debate on the American Revolution, 1761-1783,* 2nd edn., A. and C. Black, 1960.
7. Keith, A.B., *Speeches and Documents on British Colonial Policy,* Oxford University Press, 1948.
8. Madden, A.F., ed. *Imperial Constitutional Documents, 1765-1952,* Blackwood, 1953.
9. Pole, J.R. ed. *The Revolution in America, 1754-1788,* Macmillan, 1970.
10. Jensen, Merrill, ed. *American Colonial Documents to 1776, English Historical Documents,* vol. 9, Eyre & Spottiswoode, 1955.

GENERAL

11. Marshall, Dorothy, *Eighteenth-Century England,* Longmans, 1962.
12. Gershoy, Leo, *From Despotism to Revolution, 1763-1789,* Harper, 1944.
13. Watson, J. Steven, *The Reign of George III,* Oxford University Press, 1960.
14. White, R.J., *The Age of George III,* Heinemann, 1968.
15. Namier, Lewis, *The Structure of Politics at the Accession of George III,* 2nd edn., Macmillan, 1957.
16. Namier, Lewis, *England in the Age of the American Revolution,* 2nd edn., Macmillan, 1961.

Bibliography

17. Brooke, John. *The Chatham Administration, 1766-8,* Macmillan, 1956.
18. Christie, Ian R., *The End of North's Ministry*, Macmillan, 1958.
19. Donoghue, Bernard, *British Politics and the American Revolution, 1773-5,* Macmillan, 1964.
20. Guttridge, G.H., *English Whiggism and the American Revolution,* University of California Press, 1942.
21. Namier, Lewis and Brooke John, *Charles Townshend,* Macmillan, 1964.
22. Thomas, P.G.D., 'Charles Townshend and American Taxation', *English Historical Review,* vol. 83, 1968, pp. 33-41.
23. Langford, Paul, 'The Rockingham Whigs and America, 1767-1773,' in *Statesmen, Scholars and Merchants: Essays in eighteenth-century history presented to Dame Lucy Sutherland,* Oxford, 1973

BRITISH COMMERCIAL AND COLONIAL POLICY

24. Keith, A.B., *Constitutional History of the First British Empire,* Oxford University Press, 1930.
25. Harlow, Vincent T., *The Founding of the Second British Empire, 1763-1793,* Longmans, 1952-64.
26. Gipson, L.H., *The British Empire before the American Revolution,* 15 vols, Harper-Row, 1936-65.
27. Gipson, L.H., *The Coming of the Revolution, 1763-1775,* Harper-Row, 1954.
28. Dickerson, O.M., *The Navigation Acts and the American Revolution,* University of Pennsylvania Press, 1951.
29. Sosin, J.M., *Agents and Merchants: British colonial policy and the origins of the American Revolution,* University of Nebraska Press, 1965.
30. Sosin, J.M., *Whitehall and the Wilderness: the Middle West in British Colonial Policy, 1760-1775,* University of Nebraska Press, 1961.
31. Andrews, C.M., *The Colonial Period of American History,* 5 vols, Yale University Press, 1934-38.
32. Harper, L.A., *The English Navigation Laws,* New York, 1939; repr. Octagon Press, 1964.

POLITICAL DEVELOPMENT OF THE COLONIES BEFORE 1763

33. Brown, R.E., *Middle-Class Democracy and the Revolution in Massachusetts, 1691-1780,* Harper-Row, 1955; repr. Russell, 1968.

34. Wertenbaker, T.J., *Give me Liberty: the Struggle for Self-Government in Virginia,* American Philosophical Society, 1958.
35. Greene, Jack P., *The Quest for Power: The Lower Houses of Assembly in the Southern Colonies, 1689-1776,* North Carolina University Press, 1963.
36. Pole, J.R., *Political Representation in England and the Origins of the American Republic,* Macmillan, 1966.

GENERAL HISTORIES OF THE AMERICAN REVOLUTION

37. Miller, J.C., *The Origins of the American Revolution,* 2nd edn., Oxford, 1960.
38. Wright, Esmond, *Fabric of Freedom,* Macmillan, 1959.
39. Alden, J.R., *A History of the American Revolution: Britain and the Loss of the Thirteen Colonies,* Macdonald, 1969.
40. Lacy, Dan, *The Meaning of the American Revolution,* New American Library, 1964.
41. Robson, Eric, *The American Revolution,* Batchworth, 1955.

SPECIAL ASPECTS OF THE REVOLUTION

42. Arendt, Hannah, *On Revolution,* Viking Press, New York, 1963.
43. Palmer, R.R., *The Age of Democratic Revolution,* 2 vols., Princeton University Press, 1959.
44. Schlesinger, A.M., *The Colonial Merchants and the American Revolution, 1763-1776,* New York, 1918, repr. Atheneum Press, 1968.
45. Bailyn, Bernard, *The Ideological Origins of the American Revolution,* Harvard University Press, 1967.
46. Hacker, Louis M., *The Triumph of American Capitalism,* Columbia University Press, 1940.
47. Knollenburg, Bernhard, *Origins of the American Revolution, 1759-1766,* Macmillan, New York, 1960.
48. Morgan, Edmund S. and Morgan, Helen M., *The Stamp Act Crisis: Prologue to Revolution,* rev. edn., paperback, University of North Carolina Press, 1963.
49. Boorstin, Daniel J., *The Genius of American Politics,* University of Chicago Press, 1953.
50. Hartz, Louis, *The Liberal Tradition in America,* Harcourt Brace, 1955.
51. Wright, Benjamin F., *Consensus and Continuity, 1776-1787,* Norton 1958.
52. Labaree, B.W., *The Boston Tea Party,* Oxford University Press, 1964.

53. Maier, Pauline, *From Resistance to Revolution: Colonial Radicalism and the Development of American Opposition to Britain*, Routledge, 1973.
54. Olson, A.G. and Brown, R.M., *Anglo-American Political Relations, 1675-1775*, Rutgers University Press, 1970.

BIBLIOGRAPHICAL ESSAYS

55. Wright, Esmond, *The Causes and Consequences of the American Revolution*, Chicago, Watts, 1966.
56. Greene, Jack P., *The Ambiguity of the American Revolution*, Harper, 1968.
57. Christie, Ian R., 'The Historian's quest for the Revolution'. in *Statesmen, Scholars and Merchants*, Oxford University Press, 1973.
58. Christie, Ian R., *Crisis of Empire: Great Britain and the American colonies, 1754-1783*, Arnold, 1966.

Index

Index